JUST A CANDY STORE IN BROOKLYN

Or Was It?

TOM MORRISSEY

Happyful Publishing

Contents

ONE

Life in the Hook

The sun had not yet risen one April morning in 1968 on Van Brunt Street in the Red Hook section of Brooklyn, New York. The only activity at all was indicated by the lights of the small store near the corner of Dykeman Street. It was owned by John and Mary Maguire and they were busy preparing coffee and setting up the daily newspapers for sale, readying for the human deluge of local factory workers about to descend on them. They understood the dire need of their customers for morning coffee, cigarettes, and newspapers. No sane person would stand in the way of this charging herd of simple, hardworking, and mostly loving people making their way through this Brooklyn candy store and coffee shop.

Most days in Red Hook began this way and always had according to the memory of the oldest regular customer of John and Mary's, one Bill Miller. He was addressed by all as "Mister Miller," and he was somewhere near eighty years of age, give or take a year or two. He could recall people coming to this store when the Red Hook electric trolley was still running and the store was owned by the Papajonnies, an immigrant Italian family. True, the people might have changed over the years, but not their habits. Mr. Miller would come in early in the morning, shortly after opening, dressed as sharp as a tack. Sitting at the counter, he would hold court and greet everyone, who in turn greeted him. His nickname was "Moose," which was the name he fought under many years before, "when boxing was boxing." And at his age, he could still give a good account of himself if called upon to do so.

Now, some of the regular customers of John and Mary's, during and after the morning rush, were an eclectic group who will be referred to at times as the "Red Hook Mensa Society." Members of the actual Mensa society all have IQs of 150 or better. But the Mensa group at John and Mary's had a collective IQ of 150. Take Joey Fingers (the numbers guy or local bookie), called that because he was missing several fingers. He had an incredible memory and never had to write down the numbers that the gamblers (who were almost the entire population of Red Hook) played. This was an asset because the police could never get any evidence on him and therefore couldn't arrest him for illegal gambling. Then there was Lulu, a middle-aged lady who was married to a grumpy man named Lou. She seldom left the neighborhood. As a dedicated member of the Veterans of Foreign Wars Women's Auxiliary, Lulu loved the neighborhood parades put on by the Auxiliary Post on certain holidays. The "Post" was how the Veterans of Foreign Wars was known in Red Hook. She kind of marched everywhere she went. Lulu had an uncanny resemblance to the many professional boxers whose first names always seemed to be Rocky.

Next, there was Iron Jaw Joe, who could actually pull a bus with his teeth, an amazing feat for a man who was only 5'6" and weighed barely 135 lbs. Joe was one of the few people born in the United States who emigrated with his parents to Italy as a child, and when World War II broke out, he was drafted as a young adult into the Italian army (That's "Eye-talian" as per John's pronunciation and "Talian" according to Mary.) He was later captured by the Allied Forces, and when it was learned he was actually an American citizen, he was returned to America and then was subsequently drafted into the US Army. He was the only man to have fought as a member of opposing armies in the same war. Iron Jaw Joe was one of the leading members of the society and spoke with a very pronounced accent. Whenever he got excited, he would say things like "God bless America" and sometimes even swallow a lighted cigarette, washed down with coffee, to express his love of this country. (This might make sense only to native Red Hookers.) Joe would come in later in the morning, as he was in show business, in a sense. He had appeared on the *Tonight Show* many times, demonstrating his ability to lift people and pull them in buses with his teeth. He also had a nightclub act. He was a neighborhood celebrity and a faithful customer of John and Mary's.

On this particular morning of that particular day, the word in the neighborhood was that the Galucci family from President Street was going to have a word with Lefty Keegan over the way he was treating his wife, who by the way, was the goddaughter of the don Anthony Galucci, referred to as "sir" or "Don" by everyone in the neighborhood who knew better than to be stupid about the protocol. The question on the street seemed to always be "Anything happen yet?" and the answer was "Don't know." John thought the "Eye-talians" were a good bunch of people, but he wouldn't hang out with them. Mary, although she was Irish and German, could speak "Talian" fluently and was well-versed in that national tradition after having been raised in a totally Italian neighborhood. She never criticized them for any reason. She'd just say, "They have their ways . . . Salute," and she'd shrug her shoulders in a "who can explain it" manner.

"A pack a' L&Ms and a coffee, light and sweet," requested a patron to John, who grabbed a pack of L&M cigarettes from the rack, laid them on the counter, and poured a coffee that was light and sweet.

"How're ya doin', Raymundo?" John asked, smiling as he made change for the five-dollar bill presented him by the Puerto Rican factory worker who responded with a smile and then hurriedly made his way to work after saying "Okay, Jonnie . . . see you."

When the sun was up a little higher in the sky, the kids were on their way to school and massed into the store to get their candy supply for the day ahead. Mary stood guard over the candy counter, selling the loose candy to the noisy and spirited children, looking like a mother bird distributing worms to her chicks. Although she loved these kids . . . she didn't quite trust them when it came to candy.

There were dreamers and schemers that peopled John and

Mary's, and concepts and ideas were kicked around constantly by the Mensas and non-Mensas alike. There were sizes and shapes, ages and philosophies that would have caught the attention of even the most disinterested. Let's take Billy the Bird, for instance. He was a long-shoreman on workmen's compensation due to an injury he received while working on the docks. At age twenty-four he still lived with his parents, and he could be heard constantly saying things like . . . "I woulda" or "I shoulda played four-fourteen." (The daily numbers gambling game so popular in the poorer Brooklyn neighborhoods.) "I shoulda played 'Good to Go' at the track." The consummate gambler, he seemed to always regret making the wrong bet, then trying to explain to himself why.

Billy might seem a lazy sort from this description, but he really wasn't that way at all. Just put him in a challenging situation, and he instantly became the world's most focused man. He was one of those valuable assets that were designed and placed in society by a law of God that has driven mankind from the first moments of conscious-ness. He was "the dreamer." The one who could dream up the most implausible of all prospects and talk about them until someone heard his message and became the other part of the grand design . . . the "doer."

Billy's hobby was raising homing pigeons. Hence the nickname "the Bird." He sometimes, in his head, redesigned everything in his immediate environment. But now he was working on something that could make him a millionaire. Even richer than the "homin' pidgin training program" he had designed for Joey Fingers and all the other hard-pressed numbers runners (bookies) in "da city." With that program, the numbers runners (illegal betting on "numbers" that appeared daily in the newspapers) could attach the bet sheets of their customers to a homing pigeon's leg and set it free to fly to the central numbers-collection facility, which in Joey Finger's case, was the back-yard of a store on President Street owned by the Galucci family. This plan was put into action with great expectation and many of Billy's prized birds, but fell on hard times when the birds, for some strange reason, started flying to the 76th police precinct, which was just two blocks over from Galucci Family central. It should be noted that the NYPD's 76th precinct had a newly vacated rear building that had become a home away from home for many of the borough's wayward pigeons . . . most of them female. Some of the cops felt sorry for the birds and were bringing them feed. This confused Billy's birds, and the rest is history.

This threw the numbers world into total chaos and would have cost Billy at least a beating but for the fact that his mother, Janet, was a close friend of Don Galucci's wife, Teresa. They even went to bingo together, they were that close. Teresa would have nothing to do with beating up her close friend's offspring.

Billy realized he was not in good graces with the don. As a result, he began to turn his attention to another enterprise that was legal and could be very profitable: the enterprise of creature comfort. He was working on a design for a convertible sofa bed that would completely revolutionize the sleeper-sofa business. His plan was to invent the automatic sofa bed opener, which would, with the press of a button, automatically open and close the usually cumbersome sofa beds and save the backs of all those aging mothers who still had adult children living with them in four-room, cold-water flats in the great neighborhoods of that wonderful city known as New York. Four-room, cold-water flats always had only one or two bedrooms, and the "kids" had to sleep on the sofa beds. Things the kids never closed. So their mamas had to.

Don Anthony Galucci had been made aware of Billy the Bird's current interest through his wife, and it should be said that he was very interested in it. He often chided his only son Pat (many times referred to as "Fat Pat" due to his size) with words like "Why don't you invent somethin'? You go aroun' criticizing everybody, all the time. You get what I mean?"

Pat was very jealous of anyone's success, especially anyone who was praised by his father. Billy's praise was not well received by Fat Pat Galucci. It got so bad that he started grunting at the mere mention of Billy's name and would immediately start thinking, "What a dumb asshole, this guy. Even his birds are dumb (grunt) . . . Almost made the Seven Six (police precinct) our partners (grunt)." But he was interested in this new invention, as he referred to all new things mechanical. He might even be willing to give Billy a break if he would cut him in on this.

TWO

Sitting Down with the Don

Billy had been summoned to a meeting with Don Anthony Galucci at the social club on President Street that was the headquarters for the Galucci family "enterprises." He sat across from the boss, sipping a cup of espresso, listening intently to every word the man spoke before he ventured to speak about his new project, which was much farther along in development than he was letting on.

"Don Anthony, you know if I can pull this new invention off, I'll be able to make up to you for what I done with the birds," Billy the Bird told the senior Galucci as he sat upright and attentive. "I shoulda done this instead of doing the birds."

"You shoulda." The don nodded in agreement as he settled his big butt back in his chair, flicked the ash from the end of his cigar, and breathed a long breath of pseudo-relaxation. "You know, Billy," he said after he looked at him for a moment in his don-like manner, "you might be on to something here." He paused for a mafia boss–like studying of Billy. "Tell me about this invention." He took a puff on his cigar as he smiled and winked.

Billy was glad to hear him say, "If you need any money to get you started, I might be willin' ta help." He followed that with a "so-there" shrugging gesture.

"With all due respect and honor, I thank you, Don Galucci, but I think I can do it with Harold's spring." Billy looked intently at the boss, wishing that he hadn't brought Harold into the conversation. "Damn," he thought as the words rolled out of his mouth, "I shoulda not done that."

Don Galucci bolted up straight in his chair as he said angrily, "What do ya mean, Harold's spring? That Mick's a crazy asshole. And besides, he buries people for a livin'. You're telling me that you're gonna have him partner with us? No freakin' way is that gonna happen." The don was surprised and extremely annoyed.

"No, no . . . please listen." Billy was scrambling hard to keep this from going off in an impossible direction that could, in the end, leave him lying in a hospital bed somewhere. He went on with, "Harold's got this new thing he come up with. I'm tellin' ya, it's the world's strongest spring. Just the thing we need to make a fold-up sofa react to an electric signal and open and close without having to do it by hand. I don't know where he came up with a spring as strong and flexible as this, but it really can work. I, uh, *we* need it ta be able ta pull this off." Billy studied the don's face for a favorable reaction.

"What's he gonna want out of this, Billy?" came the voice of Fat Pat, who had entered the room during the conversation. He went to stand behind the seated Billy the Bird, his arms folded across his chest.

"I don't think he wants much . . . we ain't talked a deal yet. He only wants to help get it done, for now." Billy uttered quietly as he squirmed in his chair, not comfortable with Pat even being in the room.

"Oh yeah? Well, let me tell you somethin'—" Pat started to say but was interrupted by a wave of his father's hand, signaling him to be quiet.

The don straightened up in his chair. "Billy, work with the crazy bastard, and we'll take care of the deal later." Then looking at Fat Pat, he said, "And you . . . shut your mouth and keep it shut. I'm the boss here, and I'll call the shots. You unnerstand?"

He glared at his frowning son, whose eyes went to the back of Billy's head. He didn't like being talked down to like that in front of the uncomfortable Billy Guarino, whom he addressed as "the Bird."

"Yeah sure, Pop," came the clumsy reply. He was thinking about knocking Billy on his ass when he least expected it. But he knew that he couldn't due to the (what he thought was) new partnership entered into by the Galucci family. It gave Billy some standing and kept him safe, for the moment. But those moments don't last forever.

Billy continued squirming. He hated confrontations, and he was afraid of Pat Galucci, who stood four inches taller and outweighed him by over a hundred pounds.

The person they were talking about was Harold O'Reilly, the funniest funeral director who ever lived—at least in Red Hook, Brooklyn. He was the fourth generation of a family of undertakers. They had buried most of the residents of Red Hook, practically from its beginning as a town that turned into a Brooklyn neighborhood. Harold had an uncanny ability to make people laugh, even at the saddest moments, during wakes and funerals. He sometimes drew the disdaining looks of Father Maroney (Big Mike) of Visitation Catholic Church and Father Fox of Christ Chapel, the Protestant church of Red Hook, when he was accidentally or purposefully funny at the services. People started looking for Harold's comic relief, and it always seemed to come just as things were getting really sad. It was truly remarkable and usually a relief.

"Hi ya, Harold," chimed Mary Maguire as she looked up from reading the paper behind the counter when Harold O'Reilly came bouncing into the store with his tape measure dangling in his hand.

"Where's John? I thought I'd better get his numbers again. It's been a while, and you know how people can sometimes realize little body changes with age." He winked and threw his elbow in a "nudge, nudge" motion. The Maguires enjoyed his sense of humor and the way he could make even the most sour people laugh true belly laughs.

"It's good ta see ya." He smiled and sat down on one of the six counter stools. "Cup a' coffee, Mary?" he asked as he nodded his head toward the pot. "Billy the Bird been around?"

"Hey, Harold, where's your tape?" John laughed and came through the door as he returned from checking on the neighboring store owner, Jimmy "the Fruit Stand." He segued into the running joke between Harold and half the neighborhood whenever Harold ran into someone he hadn't seen for a while: he would start to measure them with his tape measure "just to make sure the coffin was going to fit perfectly." Needless to say, it sometimes backed a few of the more serious residents of Red Hook off. They would see Harold coming at them, an extended tape in his hand, with a "I know something you don't know" look on his skinny, leprechaun-like face under his red hair. Maybe a bit much, but funny just the same.

Everyone loved Harold O'Reilly . . . but they couldn't quite figure out why he did what he did for a living. Most Red Hookers thought he should have been in the movies because he was funny like Abbott and Costello and Laurel and Hardy. Maybe he wasn't tall enough for Hollywood.

"Allo, Harold . . . hows-a you been?" asked Iron Jaw Joe as he entered the store, smiling. He was always glad to see Harold . . . but not his tape. "Eh, John-a, can-a you give-a me a coffee, a-please?"

"To go or to stay?" John asked without looking up from the sink where he was rinsing out the cloth he was about to use to wipe the counter.

"Think I'm a-gonna stay and talk-a with-a Harold here." Joe slid up on the counter stool.

"You should always take it ta go 'cause you never know when it's going to be your time . . . ta go," Harold said, feigning seriousness.

Joe looked at him for a moment, not knowing whether or not to laugh. He then laughed as Mary and John broke into laughter, and he nodded his head as if to say, "Hey, it's a joke . . . a-shue, (sure) ahm a-know that."

Joe smiled as he lit a cigarette. His eyes flashed with the brightness of the match. He had a "Dali-esque" expression that equaled the great artist's intensity. But he always had a hard time being taken seriously. Maybe it was because of his short stature or because of life's circumstance, but people always treated him like a lovable clown. He fought that image, but his struggle only seemed to make the image deeper. After all, he had appeared on national TV. And many times at that, but still the image persisted. Perhaps it was because he wasn't an intelligent man. But then again, who in this neighborhood was intelligent? Well . . . maybe Father Maroney and Father Fox . . . and . . . Harold O'Reilly. They were the only people in the neighborhood who had actually been to college. Hey, you can't forget Mr. Lynch, the high school teacher . . . He had been to college too. But that was it. No one else that he knew of, at least from Red Hook, had graduated college. Maybe he should go to college—then he would be ranked up there with these four guys. Then again, he couldn't do that because he never even graduated elementary school. So much for that idea.

"Billy the Bird was a-telling us about-a you spring . . . " Iron Jaw Joe said nonchalantly.

"He was? What did he say about it?" asked Harold as he swallowed a mouthful of coffee. "Did he tell you how I tested it?" He stood up a moment to brush some crumbs from his black pants. His thin frame and five-foot-eight height made him look like he came out of a Barry Fitzgerald movie when the light hit him right, and at other times, he looked like the undertaker that he was.

John was looking over the scratch sheet, (horse-racing form) which he had lying in front of him on the counter, getting ready to decide on which horses he was going to bet on that day through his bookie. Without looking away from the paper, he asked Harold casually, "Have you tested that spring of yours out on anything?"

"Not in any way that would prove what it really can do. But I'm always looking for a safe way to test it. You got any ideas, John?"

John looked up from the scratch sheet and paused for a moment. "Maybe you could get yourself a horse and attach a spring to its ass. Then, when they put him in the gate, back him up to the rear gate far enough so that when they open the front gate, the horse will jump out ahead of the rest of them and maybe even break track records." He laughed heartily, loving the picture he was seeing in his head.

"I like it, John." Harold took a sip of his coffee. "You do good with the ponies, John?"

John chuckled good-naturedly. "The last horse I bet on yesterday, well . . . They're still lookin' for him." It seemed John's horses never did "come in." They ran but seldom, if ever, won.

It was a fact that John's focus was always on Mary. Next it was on his three kids, who were all grown and living their lives with careers in other parts of the country. Then came his bookie, followed by the scratch sheet. John was an easygoing, older man who had been born in Virginia, went to sea in his late teens, then met Mary while on shore leave in Brooklyn in an ice cream parlor (neither of them frequented bars). Since she had never been outside of Brooklyn, she was swept off her feet by this world traveler, John Maguire. They married when she was twenty and he was twenty-eight, and they settled in Red Hook. Mary wanted him home with her, so he could no longer go to sea. He went to work in Todd's Shipyard, which was a major company in the shipbuilding business. In his earlier years, he had been told that he resembled Bing Crosby. But as he aged, he became almost a double for the actor Jimmy Cagney. John liked looking like these men because he saw them as good men, and he considered himself a good man . . . and he certainly was. Leaving the sea that he loved so much had been a struggle for him, but it was worth it to have Mary by his side, as his wife. It was probably the horse betting that helped take the edge off losing the salt water and sailing all over the world.

Mary was born fighting. She battled something every day of her life. As a child, she battled school. She never liked going to school. As an adolescent, she battled her mother's strictness, and as an adult, she battled anyone who tried to get over on her. And she loved every minute of every battle she had ever fought. When she met John, for the first time in her life she had no need to fight. He was polite, handsome, and very easygoing. He had actually been out of Brooklyn and even out of the country, and he wasn't swell-headed about it at all. Although he did speak funny (a bit of a Southern accent), his soft-spoken manner made up for it.

They struggled with poverty in their early years of marriage and raised three children as life got better—until John came down with emphysema, and he had to retire from Todd's Shipyard. They bought a candy store that became a Red Hook success story.

"Hey, Harold . . . how are ya?" asked Billy "the Bird" Guarino as he entered the store, smiling. "Hi, John . . . Hi, Mary . . . Hey, Joe. And what is it?"

Before he could sit down, Harold gushed, "I brought the new spring . . . Billy." He was grinning broadly. "But you know what? I think I want to try it out at work first." He nodded in support of what he thought was a good idea. "Uh, before you put it through the mill."

"How you gonna do that? Put it in one of the stiffs?" Billy asked as he settled onto the counter stool.

"You never know," answered Harold over his coffee cup, chuckling.

"I don't like that, Harold," Mary said with mock caution. "The last time you chuckled like that was when you scared the hell out of the cleaning lady at the funeral parlor when you popped out of the coffin she was dusting."

"Oh, yeah. And she's probably still running as a result." He laughed, enjoying the memory.

"She's-a no think that was-a funny too long, Harold," chimed in Joe. "And her boyfriend, he's-a still look for you. He's-a pissed off over it."

Harold's face filled with mischief "She thought it was a real ghost, and I told her boyfriend that I didn't know what he was talking about. He's just mad that she peed her pants on the way out of the parlor and then caught a cold on the run home."

"You're heartless, Harold," Billy opined as he laughed. He remembered how Harold used to play jokes even on the good Sisters of Saint Joseph when he and Harold were in the same class way back in Visitation Parish Elementary School.

They all loved a practical joke at John and Mary's, especially Harold's, except of course when the joke was on them. But in the end, wasn't Harold's final joke on all of them?

Billy took the spring out of Harold's hand. He half whistled while he studied it from all sides. "This is it, huh? This is what's gonna make us rich. Looks like a thousand other springs I saw before."

"Billy, my boy, this spring could launch you into space if placed right, of course. I have one or two more tests of it to conduct, then we'll be ready to go." Harold sounded very convincing. Well, why wouldn't he? For as he was known throughout Red Hook, because of his actually going to college he now was "as smart as shit."

Billy agreed with, "Okay, Harold, but this needs to be in place and ready to go by Christmas, or there might be a problem."

"What problem? Somebody gonna beat us out?"

"You never know." Billy answered with a shrug as Harold made a mental note to explore that thought. As far as he was concerned, they were in on the bottom floor of something that was going to make them both filthy rich. This was going to revolutionize the sofa bed industry. In his head was the thought "Watch out world—because here come the two guys from Red Hook with a product that will rock the world even more than the other Red Hook product, White Rock Soda." A solid company that had gone nationwide and was based in the neighborhood at the foot of Beard Street, sitting right on the water's edge.

THREE

The Problem with Harold

Harold O'Reilly had indeed stumbled onto some things that could make him a very rich man. One of them was this spring of his that was so powerful and flexible that it could not only make the automatic sofa bed concept a reality but it could also quite probably revolutionize the auto industry, the elevator industry, and even the circus. And who could ever imagine a car with suspension springs so robust yet compact that they could make a car ride smooth to the point of making one think that he or she were on a boat or plane and lighten that car by two hundred pounds? Then just think of how much easier and faster elevator doors could open and close. And how about circus daredevils being shot out of spring-loaded cannons twice as fast and far as ever before? The world would truly be a different place. Harold set about planning his test of "the world's most awesome spring," and he didn't care what it would take to measure this magnificent innovation.

Meanwhile on President Street, a conversation about the same subject was taking place between Pat Galucci and his father. "Pop, ya know I've been thinking a lot about this invention that Billy the Bird

is inventin', and I'm getting a little worried about the ⟨
buddying up with this Harold guy."

His father sat behind his desk in the back of the Galucci ⟨⟨⟨⟨⟨,
storefront and social club, reading the *Daily News*. The senior Galucci
didn't look over the paper at his son but said with a puff of cigar
smoke slowly drifting out of his mouth, "So you been thinking, huh?
You've had a bug up your ass with Billy the Bird since you guys was
kids, and you wanna know somethin'? I don't know why. He's such a
puny little bastard, and he don't bother no one. And you got this
thing about him." He then lowered the paper and stared at his son,
who was starting to wish he had kept his mouth shut. The don
continued, "You jealous a' him or somethin'? You better understand,
he is on to what could be uncredible with this sofa thing, and I want
us to help him and be his partners. I don't want you pushing him
around or getting in his way." He paused for a moment. "Let me
know that you do understand that. Do I gotta say more?" He kept his
focus on his son to make his point.

"But, Pop . . . I know what you're saying and I respect that . . .
really. But this guy, he's tied in with this Harold O'Reilly, who you
know is half a loon, don't you? And besides . . . I don't think we need
him," the younger Galucci said confidently. "He's not blood. He's
nothin' but an undertaker, and he's Irish, so you know he probably
hits the juice hard."

"Billy said he needs him for his spring, and that's what will make
the sofa open and close . . . almost by itself." The don pointed his
finger at his son. "You don't get that he is the guy who really invented
the spring, do ya? I'm hearing that he come up with a new formula
for making it so freakin' powerful that it can change the whole world
of springs. Do you unnerstand what's going on here? Please tell me
you do." His exasperation was beginning to show.

"A spring's a spring," the younger Galucci replied, with a "what's
the difference?" shrug. "I can go to the hardware store and buy a
spring that does the same thing that this crazy bastard's spring
can do."

"You can go to the hardware store and buy a spring that will do
the same thing as his spring," the elder Galucci repeated slowly. He
put the paper down and said with annoyance showing in his tone, "If

it is that simple, I want you to get up off your fat ass and go to the store and buy a spring and bring it to Billy the Bird and get this sofa bed thing done so we can sell it. But if your idea don't work, then I want you to shut your mouth and let these two assholes finish this so we all can make some money . . . Capeesh?"

"Yeah, okay, Pop . . . I'm gonna do just that . . . and maybe you'll see what I'm talkin' about." Pat headed out the door and put his six-foot, two-hundred-and-fifty-pound frame into his Cadillac and headed for Stadermann's hardware store. He had always hated it when his father demeaned him by not even listening to him when he had an idea. Especially a good one like this. And here he was doing it again by taking Billy the Bird's plan and accepting it as absolute truth, not even giving his own son a chance to get in on the action. This was the way it was all the years that he was a kid. Now here he was, a grown man, still being treated the same way. He thought about how he always seemed to be out of sync with his father's views on almost everything, yet he knew his father loved him. But his mother? Now that was a different story. Yeah, everything he did was okay with that wonderful woman. She always praised him and told him that maybe one day he'd be the first Italian-American president of the United States. Then he found himself wondering why there had never been an Italian-American in the White House. "Probably," he thought, "it was because some Mick bastards don't want it that way. But they'd probably let a loony tune like Harold O'Reilly be president before him just because he's not Italian. Where's the justice? Harold? What a jerk!" He tensed his face with the thought. "I would make a great president! Just think of the broads I'd have around me if I was the president."

Harold was at his makeshift lab in the funeral parlor, filling the spring mold with a new and improved alloy that he hoped would perform even better than the one he was presently testing. He had his laboratory set up next to the embalming room . . . so he knew he would have privacy. Because who in their right mind would come snooping around a place where there were dead bodies?

Billy was working on the push button control that would initiate the folding-out-and-in process for the world's first automatic sofa bed. Think of all the mothers who would be so appreciative of him for being freed from the labor of folding up the couch every day and opening it every night. Finally, he would be appreciated! He would be somebody people could look up to. He could almost hear fathers telling their kids, "Hey, why can't you be more like that guy Billy the Bird from Red Hook?" He thought to himself, "Yeah, I like that. Be more like Billy the Bird from Red Hook." It made him feel good as he continued with his development of the control for the automatic opener and closer. He was a truly happier person because of that bit of fantasizing.

"What kind of spring is it that you want?" asked Mr. Stadermann with a puzzled look on his face. Stadermann was the owner of the only hardware store in Red Hook and the place where he had conducted business for many of the seventy years of his time on the planet. He was close friends with Bill "Moose" Miller, who was at that moment looking for a new lock for his cellar door as Stadermann waited on the younger Galucci's answer.

"Uh, one that will be powerful enough to open and close a sofa coach by itself. You know, somethin' with a lot of snap in it," he answered, well pleased with what he thought was a witty answer.

Mr. Stadermann studied Pat for a moment and scratched his head. Then he asked, "Something with 'snap'? Hmmm. What kind of spring? I need to know the dimensions, the torque. How long and how wide do you want it?"

"Uh, I don't really know. I guess it's gotta be strong enough to open a coach and small enough to fit inside of it." A "What do you want from me?" hand gesture accompanied his words and attitude. Pat was easily frustrated by questions for which he had no answers. He shrugged his shoulders and turned his back on Mr. Stadermann while pretending to look out the store window onto Van Brunt Street. He watched Stadermann's reflection in the window glass as he began the process of searching for several springs to show him.

"Okay, let me take a look," said the pleasant old German-American who looked like he was a granddad to the whole world. He shook his snow-white head as he walked toward the spring shelf. He touched his temple and made a circle with his finger, indicating he was dealing with a man who had a screw loose.

"I saw that, Mister Stadermann," Pat said menacingly as he spun around to face the old man.

"You saw what? The spring?" asked Stadermann, looking back at him, squinting.

"No, I just seen what you did with your finger." He was starting to get angry, which was not unusual, and getting into his threatening mode when Moose Miller walked toward the counter.

"What's your problem?" he asked as he stared Pat down.

"I'm getting pissed here . . . I come into this old asshole's store and I ask for a spring, and he treats me like I'm some kinda fool. And I don't like it," Pat complained as he leaned across the counter, staring at the befuddled Mr. Stadermann, who shook his head in confusion.

"Who are you calling an asshole? Asshole!" Miller spewed into the angry man's face.

"What? You're gonna get into this now?" Pat fired back.

"I'm already in." Moose Miller leaned forward as he balled his fists. "I'm going to ask you again, who are you calling an asshole?" Pat had heard what a badass Miller was, and although he thought he could take him easily, he didn't want his father "jumping him" for duking it out with an old guy.

Mr. Stadermann hurriedly brought him a spring, hoping to quell the tension. "Here is one that will probably do the trick for you." He laid it on the counter directly in front of the red-faced Galucci.

"Do the trick, huh? Well it better, or I'll be back," he said menacingly as he threw two dollars on the counter and picked up the spring, studying it for a moment.

"And you'd better bring some friends with you," advised Miller.

"Bring my friends? Why?" Pat was puzzled.

"To help carry you out of here when I get done with you."

"Yeah, and that's supposed to scare me, old man." Pat chuckled with a slight grin on his face.

"I think that right now you're about to piss your pants. So why don't you put your fat ass out that door and keep it that way until you learn some respect for us 'old' guys." Moose Miller kept his gaze fixed on the younger Galucci as he backed toward the door.

"Remember what I said." Pat held the spring above his head, shaking it. "If this doesn't work, I'll be bringing it back."

"Try putting it up your ass and see if that works," grumbled Miller as the young mobster exited the store.

Pat Galucci gunned the engine of his Cadillac and headed back to President Street, which was five minutes away. While he drove, he envisioned himself a very rich man with a bevy of beautiful showgirls surrounding him. He squirmed around in the seat and got into a comfortable, "manly" position. He chuckled and thought that he would one day have his own driver and travel anywhere he wanted, and everyone would have to treat him with respect when he got there. He liked this thought and filed it into his fantasy daydream memory bank.

FOUR

The Hidden

A week later, Lulu fumbled with her purse for the keys to the door to Bill Miller's house as she waited for her coffee to-go at John and Mary's. She was his housekeeper and was paid by the old gentleman to do his housework, cook a few meals, do his laundry . . . and keep an eye out for him. She had not seen him for a few days, and when she asked Mary if they had seen him come into the candy store, the answer was no. That was unusual.

"We bet on a horse together the other day. The horse won and paid good, so he's got some money coming. You should go and tell him I've got it for him," John said as he poured water in the coffee machine.

"It's not like him to not come around for a few days. Maybe he's sick, Lulu." Mary's voice indicated concern.

"I'm going down there right now. I'll tell him you're worried about him. He'll like hearing that." Lulu turned and headed out the store, marching her way to "Mister" Miller's, a few blocks away. As she walked, she thought about how long she had known him. When she was a child, he was the hero of Red Hook to all the kids in the neighborhood. He was the best boxer she had ever seen, and he never got "stuck up" because of it either. Her father was a fan of Moose Miller, and he didn't usually like anybody who wasn't Italian.

Especially in the boxing ring. She thought about the old fighter standing up to people who were always trying to bully around the little guys and old people.

She recalled the time when Fat Pat Galucci and his dumb friends were teasing Jimmy the Fruit Stand and started getting cruel with him. Jimmy told them to knock it off and made a fist like he was gonna punch one of them. Pat got way out of hand, lost his temper, and made for Jimmy, grabbing him by the shirt collar. Now, Jimmy was an older man who had run his fruit store for many years, and he never hurt anyone. He took in every stray animal in the neighborhood and besides, he was all bent over.

It had all started when Pat's friend got into a difference of opinion with Jimmy over a pair of shoes Jimmy had sold him the week before. They were teasing him about selling shoes in a fruit store. Jimmy told them it was hard enough making a living, and he didn't want to be bothered by the likes of them over his shoe business. The commotion brought Mr. Miller over from John and Mary's two stores away, where he was having his daily coffee. He had that killer look in his eye when he entered the fruit store, and even though he was way older, Pat was scared shitless of him.

"What's going on here?" grumbled Moose Miller, looking intently at Pat.

At first no one said a word as Pat backed off his grip on Jimmy.

"Let's go . . . this guy's too touchy. Why, we was only having a little fun with him, and he gets all pissed off," Pat complained as he started to move out the door.

"He ain't no punching bag for little humps like you guys. He's an old man and you leave him alone . . . Understand?" Bill Miller glared as he spoke almost in a whisper.

"You're an old man," said Pat's friend Junior with a chuckle. "What about it, Pat?" He poked Pat in the arm.

"I'm still young enough to wipe the street with the likes a' you," came Bill Miller's reply. He cocked his chin, which was usually a signal that he was getting ready to let one go.

Junior looked at Pat, who was signaling for them to leave. They did so because he didn't want his father getting word that he had messed up some old man. Then there was the other consideration: he didn't want to suffer the humiliation of getting his ass kicked by the legendary Red Hook boxer. Sure, he was old, but this guy could hit harder than anyone he knew, who were mostly half his age, and Pat didn't want to take any chances.

Lulu was so proud of her hero Mr. Miller that day over something that had happened a few years before. She rattled the keys in her hand as she started up the small stoop leading to his front door, and after a moment of fumbling with them, she got control of the situation and opened the door. She knew something was wrong immediately because all of the lights were on, and Mr. Miller never used lights during the day. She called his name as she rounded the corner from the hallway. Going into the living room, she gasped as she came upon the lifeless body sitting upright in his easy chair with the newspaper on his lap. His head was back, eyes staring at the ceiling. Moose Miller had moved on.

As with just about everybody in Red Hook, Bill "Moose" Miller wound up at the funeral home where Harold and family prepared him for burial. He was waked there for two days, and everybody from the neighborhood and beyond came to pay their respects. It was quite a gathering. The first night, Iron Jaw Joe came with his family and lost no time telling everybody that Bill Miller was the bravest man he ever knew. Joey Fingers, the bookie, said Bill Miller was the best horse player he ever knew. John and Mary told many war stories about Bill Miller and focused on the one about the time he rescued Jimmy the Fruit Stand from Pat "you know who" and his "asshole friends." Jimmy the Fruit Stand nodded his agreement as Mary told the story. She was a very animated person, especially when telling stories she liked.

Harold O'Reilly stood silently by, drinking this all in, thinking about what a jerk Pat Galucci was and how nice it would be to have him as the subject of one of his grand practical jokes. Yes, indeed. Yes, *indeed!*

Pat Galucci screeched his car's brakes whenever he wanted to be noticed, and funerals and wakes were no exception to this. He lumbered out from behind the wheel as he exited his Caddy. Junior, his friend and stooge, got out from the passenger side, buttoning the jacket of his sharkskin-gray suit and adjusting his black tie "out of respect for the dead." With his dark hair slicked down atop his ratty face and lanky, thirty-year-old body, he looked like a skinny kid who was on his way to confession at church as he hurried around the rear of the car. He walked a little behind Fat Pat because that was what you did in Red Hook when walking with the boss's kid.

As they entered the funeral parlor, they ran into the "Friendly Undertaker" himself.

"Hey, Harold, my father said I should tell you he will cover anything left that's not paid for with Old Man Miller's funeral." Pat gestured toward the coffin lying in the front of the room. "He said he'll be here tomorrow night to pay his respects. You should just let him know then if there's any uncovered expenses."

"That's very nice of him. And nice of you. Oh, and of course . . . you too, Junior." Harold was always very polite, but his mind was working all the time. His mind was really rolling at that point. "But his insurance is covering everything. But my thanks to your dad just the same."

"Billy the Bird here yet?" Pat asked as he walked into the lobby.

"No, but half the neighborhood is. They're all over the place. Just take a look." He gestured toward the viewing room and then the waiting area, which was not in full sight from where they were standing because it was blocked by the wall they were standing near.

Pat moved away from Harold, looked inside, nodded his head to everyone, who nodded back, not wanting to piss him off by ignoring him. He motioned to Junior to follow him over to a corner where they could talk without being overheard.

"Where is it you think this asshole keeps his laboratory?" Pat asked in a low voice as Junior shrugged his shoulders in a "how should I know" gesture.

Harold was watching them and wondering what they were talking about. He couldn't help but notice that they were avoiding eye contact with him as they huddled. He chuckled when they moved toward the back area of the funeral parlor and bumped into his father, John O'Reilly, who was coming out of his office.

"Oh, how are you, Mister O?" asked an uncomfortable and a bit surprised Pat.

"Hello . . . the wake area is over there." Harold's father was a red-faced, burly man with a shock of white hair. He pointed toward the room where Moose Miller lay in his coffin, thinking that they were somehow lost in the crowd.

"Uh, yeah, I know . . . but I was looking for the rest room. Funerals make me pee a lot. For some reason." He chuckled quietly, thinking he was being funny. Pat was trying to hide his fear of dead bodies by attempting to be glib while avoiding going near Bill Miller's body. His nightmares were frequently about dead people suddenly coming back to life and chasing him. But he was also trying to get a make on where Harold kept his laboratory, and now he thought he would have to do some undercover work to find it. If he could find it, then maybe he could learn how Harold made the spring or maybe even get lucky and steal one so he would be able to get it duplicated. Or maybe even find a written formula for it.

Billy the Bird came in to pay his respects to Mr. Miller and started talking with Harold. Pat went over to him, grabbed his arm, and took him aside. "Listen, Billy . . . you been talking about this spring that Harold's invented, and it's supposed to be so wonderful and all . . . Well, I got this here one"—he pulled the spring he bought at Stadermann's hardware store from his suit jacket's inside pocket— "and I think if you try this, it might work. And then we can start getting this thing on the road." He looked at Billy in a slightly menacing way. The Bird did not want to make any trouble with Pat, especially there, so he said, "Okay, Pat, we'll have a look."

Galucci grabbed him on his arm and leaned into him, eye-to-eye. "*We'll?* What's with this 'we'll' shit?"

"Oh . . . I mean, I'll have a look at it. It probably will work . . . I bet it will," Billy said, glad that Pat had relaxed his grip on his arm as he moved away.

Harold watched as Pat then made a quick exit with Junior following closely behind. He walked over to Billy. "You okay, Billy?"

"Yeah, yeah . . . I'm fine, Harold, but that guy is trouble. Could be big trouble for us," Billy said, regaining his composure. He was afraid of Pat, and he was never able to stand up for himself against him—or anybody else, for that matter—ever since he was a kid. He just couldn't get anyone to respect him for who he was. He thought it was his size: short and skinny. He had no muscles but then, neither did Pat. That guy had weight, and a lot of it, but no muscles.

An idea popped into Harold's head, which had to do with his sense of Pat Galucci's fear of Moose Miller and the possibility of that fear lingering even after the old man had passed on. A slight smile broke upon his lips as the wheels began turning in his head. It was almost as if he were reading Pat's mind at that moment.

Outside the funeral parlor, Pat pointed to the building and said to Junior, "I want you to go back in there and find somewhere to hide. Then I want you to let me in at around eleven or so, when nobody's around. Ya hear?"

"What? Are you nuts?" said a disbelieving Junior. "You gotta be kiddin' me or somethin'. Me, in there by myself, with a bunch of stiffs?"

"Yeah . . . you in there with a bunch of stiffs . . . and me . . . eventually." Pat chuckled. "I need you to do this so we can all get rich. That's all I'm gonna say, but I mean this . . . Get your ass back inside and somehow disappear."

Junior straightened his tie and shook his head, but he knew there was no use arguing. What Pat Galucci wanted, Pat Galucci got. That was it. He watched the big man pull away, squealing his tires, then turned and with his bopping-bouncing, pigeon-like walk, went back inside. No one was watching his re-entry, and he slipped toward the direction of the men's room. On the way he noticed a door, and when he opened it, he discovered a closet. He took a deep breath and slid inside. Using his cigarette lighter, he looked around for a place to hide and did so behind a big barrel that was near a wall. It was empty, so he moved it with little effort and then sat down behind it, hoping the time would go quickly. He was not comfortable with this at all. He thought that no one had seen him as he pulled this off. And no one had . . . Well, almost no one.

Many of the residents of Red Hook came by to pay their respects that night. Father Maroney was due in the next night to say the Rosary, and everyone who was there would be back to say the Rosary with him.

Everyone filed out at nine o'clock as Harold bid them goodnight.

Iron Jaw Joe said as he was leaving, "What's up with-a that Pat Galucci? He's-a act a-funny."

"He's an asshole, Joe . . . and he's always been an asshole." Harold observed Joe's discomfort.

"I'm-a think-a that he's-a up to somethin'. He's always picking on everybody. He's-a almost put Mister Stadermann's lights out over-a somethin' as a-stupid as a spring," Joe said, shaking his head.

"A spring?" Harold felt the hair stand up on his neck when he heard this. Picking on Stadermann was bad enough, but what about this thing with a spring? The funeral director was starting to figure this all out. He thought, "Why, Pat Galucci . . . you supreme piece of shit." A knowing grin crossed Harold's face.

FIVE

In the Still of the Night

Junior sat perfectly still in the darkness of the closet, hoping no one would discover him and trying to come up with an excuse if they did. "I wonder if I told them I was hiding from Pat because I had really screwed up and he was looking to kill me? That might work, yeah, it just might."

He heard people shuffling out the door and Harold bidding them good night. Then he heard someone whistling from somewhere nearby, who he felt had to be Harold. He was sure that Harold was going to look in the closet, but he didn't. He waited breathlessly as the whistling stopped and all was totally silent. Yet he knew that there was someone still there because he didn't hear the door close, which would indicate that everyone had left for the night. This was real creepy. He thought that maybe he was being made a patsy again by his young gangster boss. "He wouldn't be caught dead in this place." The thought made him chuckle. He made a funny, accidentally, but also . . . on purpose.

He heard someone who had resumed whistling walking by the closet. It was too dark for him to see the time on his watch, but he thought it must be about ten o'clock, and the little Mick was still there. He didn't want Fat Pat to run into him and start some shit and then get them in trouble for burglary or something. Then he heard the clock chime one . . . two . . . three. He counted on his fingers up to ten when it stopped. It was ten o'clock. Pat would be there in an hour and would act like it was Junior's fault if Harold were still there. The seconds ticked away, and he started feeling sweat beads building up on his skinny forehead over his bushy, black eyebrows. He was growing more fearful by the minute, and he hoped that Harold wasn't going to sleep at the place tonight. What a crazy thought. Who sleeps in funeral homes? Maybe this guy was the one who did. It would just be his luck.

Suddenly he heard the door open and then close loudly. Then absolute silence as he continued to sit breathless in the darkness, waiting for another sound. But after a few minutes, it didn't come. He stood up and moved quietly toward the closet door. He opened it slowly and then peered out into the hall. A chill went up his spine as he realized where he was . . . again. He walked out into the hallway and paused, listening for a sound, really hating the fact that he was there. What kind of shit did Pat think he was pulling? He protested Pat's lack of consideration.

He thought he heard something from behind him, and as he whirled around to see what it was, he slipped and fell flat on his ass. Nothing was there. He got to his feet and laughed at himself for being so stupid. Yet he had the eerie feeling that there was someone standing behind him. He again spun around quickly, hoping that there wasn't anyone there. There wasn't. He let out a sigh before walking over to the entrance, where he was comforted by the sight of the streetlight shining through the glass door. He waited in the shadows for what seemed an eternity, then was startled as Pat showed up from out of nowhere outside and peered in through the glass.

Junior went quickly to open the door. "I thought you were never gonna get here," he complained.

"What are ya talking about? I couldn't just come in until I saw Harold leave for sure. And not double back." Pat motioned him to follow as they made their way toward the back of the funeral parlor. "Man, I'm glad Old Man Miller is dead. I wouldn't want to have to finally kick his ass if he found us." He laughed as he shook his head and shrugged his shoulders.

"I remember when you had the chance to really kick his ass. I guess you gave him a break, right?" responded Junior sarcastically.

"Like the beating I'm gonna put on you if you keep up with the fresh mouth." Pat was annoyed at his henchman.

They walked lightly into the funeral parlor and passed the coffin containing Moose Miller. Pat looked at it and laughed uncomfortably.

"What are you laughing at?" Junior asked quietly.

"Him. I'm having the last laugh and I'm really enjoying it," he said with a sneer that suddenly turned to a look of terror as the body of Moose Miller started to rise—slowly at first then somewhat faster—into a sitting position in the coffin.

Pat lost his balance, he was so frightened, and fell toward the coffin. Unbelievably, Moose Miller's hand raced to Pat's face as he landed one right on Galucci's cheek. The big man fell to the floor and then pushed himself away from the coffin with his feet as he screamed at the now risen body of the old warrior.

Junior shouted unintelligible words as he put his hands in front of his face, falling away from the risen body.

"Holy shit!" they yelled in unison. Pat regained his footing as they raced for the door, which they couldn't get open right away. They panicked and screamed as they finally got out the door and raced into the street shouting, "A ghost, a ghost! That old son of a bitch is still moving!"

Lights started coming on and windows were opening up and down King Street as people tried to see what was going on.

Pat raced to his car, and Junior sprinted up the block and onto Van Brunt Street, running as fast as his legs could carry him. He didn't look back. Eventually Pat caught up with him and told him to get in the car, but he just kept running and screaming, "I just seen a ghost! I just seen a ghost! Holy shit, I just seen a ghost!"

Pat pulled the car in front of him, and luckily there was no traffic at all. The streets of Red Hook were usually empty at that time of night.

"What the hell was that?" asked a terrified Junior as he got in the car and slammed the door.

"Come on, we gotta calm down here. This is nuts. The old guy is dead. Maybe it was rigor mortis or something. He's dead. You know that. Come on, take a breath, Junior." Pat tried to help calm down his hysterical underling.

"Pat . . . he rose up and hit you in your stupid jaw. He punched you."

"Don't you think I know that? Asshole."

"I was locked in there with him for the past two hours. Suppose he woulda cornered me in that closet. He would have got me and nobody would have known what happened to me." Junior was beside himself. "A friggin' living and breathing dead man. I never been so scared in my life. Holy shit!"

They would have both been beside themselves with rage if they had seen Harold at that moment, back at the funeral parlor, gently removing the spring and the board that was under the body of Mr. Miller. He then gingerly removed the spring-powered sleeve he had placed under the dead man's suit jacket. The Friendly Undertaker was laughing as he apologized to the old gent, knowing that, somewhere, he too was probably laughing his ass off right then.

"We got that asshole. Didn't we, Moose?" Harold said before he carried the spring-powered equipment back into his laboratory room from where he had observed through his one-way mirror the two hapless gangsters without either of them having an inkling that he was doing so. What Pat and Junior didn't realize was that there was a little-noticed side door into the funeral parlor where Harold had silently re-entered the building. He had picked up on something strange going on with Junior as he quietly weaseled his way around the building during the Miller wake. He watched Pat leave the wake without Junior, and the rest was history. That set into motion the plan to "reanimate" the body of Moose Miller.

SIX

For It Was Mary, Mary

"Honest, Mary . . . I just found it in the street." "Goo Goo" Bolzano said, nodding his head toward the place on Van Brunt Street where he claimed he found the box of cartons of Camel cigarettes that he was holding in his arms. "It's yours for twenty bucks. That's it."

Before she could answer, John said sternly as he stood with his hands on his hips behind the counter, "No, we don't want no stolen goods in here. You know that, Goo Goo. Come on."

"John, ya gotta listen. I honestly saw this fall right off a big truck as it turned the corner onta Sullivan Street. I suddenly ran over to grab it, so's no one got hurt driving into it, and stuff like that." He thought he was getting over on Mary. But he wasn't, as he continued his story with "Ya know I could sell these to people on my own, but that would put me in competition with you, an' I would never wanna do that. John? Mary? Come on. Do the right thing here, like I'm doing the right thing."

John didn't hesitate in his response. "Goo Goo, we're doing the right thing. No stolen merchandise sold here. Sorry, kid."

"Okay. I'll see if maybe Old Lady Meyers might be interested in 'em." He left the store, obviously disappointed and bound for Meyer's candy store, three blocks away.

"Why didn't you take them?" asked Sal Marino as he sipped his coffee, hunched over the counter. "That was a good deal." Sal was a member of the Red Hook Mensa Society, in good standing. He was a slight man in his mid-fifties who was nicknamed "Dr. No" due to his negative outlook on life. "No" was his favorite word, and whenever any of the regulars in John and Mary's wanted a negative answer to a question, they could always count on Sal.

"No dice," responded John. "I take those cigarettes, and the next thing you know, I'll have every light-fingered person in the Hook at our doorstep, wanting to sell us something they lifted. You know how that works."

Mary agreed with her husband. "I think we would have cops living in this place with their hands out if we did that."

"Yeah, I guess you're right, but it still sounds like a great deal to me. But then, what do I know?"

"Sal . . . Good deals ain't always the ones you should go with." John counseled his negative customer. "I got a guaranteed deal on a horse I wound up betting on. It didn't turn out." He straightened out the newspapers on the newsstand to the right of the door.

"Did the horse win?"

"They're still looking for him," John responded dryly.

"Who told ya it was a good deal?"

"Hat Pin Mary." John stopped what he was doing after he spoke.

"Hat Pin Mary?" Sal seemed surprised by John's answer. "She don't know nothin' about horses, John."

"Yeah, I know that now." John smiled, recalling his reason for following the eccentric lady's advice. He told Sal the rest of the story. "She had just helped the Super Swedish Angel win the heavyweight wrestling championship of the world after telling me to bet on him. And I won a few sheckles on that one."

"You know wrestling's all fixed, John. Don't tell me you don't know that." Sal waved his hand at John in mock dismissal.

"Sure I know it, but I wasn't gonna tell her that."

"Why not?" Dr. No scowled a bit.

"How do you think she helped the Angel win the match?"

Sal thought for a minute before answering, a puzzled look on his weathered face.

"Well?" John pushed for an answer.

"She probably bribed . . . uh, who was it he was wrestling?" Sal answered and asked.

"It was Gorgeous George," John responded, shaking his head and grinning.

"I don't believe that Hat Pin Mary could in any way know anything about how that match would turn out. And that you would use that as a reason for listening to her about betting a horse."

John said coyly, "So . . . here's what made me think I could trust her instincts on the horses. During the match, George had the Angel pinned, and just when it looked like it was all over . . . Mary slides over from her seat in the front row to the part of the ring where all the action was taking place, right on the ropes, where it always is in wrestling, and she sticks Gorgeous George square in the ass with her pin. The ref acts like he didn't see a thing, but it causes George to lose his grip, and the Angel comes up, flipping George and then pinning him for the count."

"And you're gonna tell me what that has to do with her instincts?" Sal asked the candy store owner.

"Here's the answer . . . or maybe I'll ask you a question about it." John leaned toward Sal with a big, knowing grin on his full, Irish face. "Maybe she didn't bribe George." John paused, awaiting Sal's answer. When none came, he volunteered, "She bribed the freakin' referee."

Sal made a face before responding. "Still ain't getting why you followed her advice on the ponies all because of a bullshit wrestling match and a crooked ref. What's with her instincts?" Sal pressed him, shrugging his skinny shoulders.

"She knew enough about that sport to know who to bribe . . . is all I'm sayin' here."

"And?" Sal asked, waiting frustratedly for the answer to his original question.

"So why wouldn't she know who to bribe at the track?" John professed.

Sal couldn't help but laugh at the response, feeling like he had been had by the old candy man's quiet sense of humor.

Hat Pin Mary was another member of the Red Hook Mensa Society, which of course met officially each day in John and Mary's candy store. She was "as crazy as bat shit," according to the local pundits. Nobody wanted to draw her wrath, which came in the form of a stick in the ass with a rather large-sized hat pin. There was a story that went around the neighborhood that the old girl was very beautiful once upon a time, back when she worked as a riveter at the Brooklyn navy yard. It was during the Big War when she fell in love with a sailor whom she had met on the job. It was a short-lived love affair but one that she would carry in her heart through all the years thereafter. They were as close as bugs in a rug for the five months that they were together, vowing unending love to one another as they filled their free time with each other. Then he shipped out suddenly one day, leaving her with a strange gift: his dead mother's distinctive hat pin. That was it. Not a ring or a necklace . . . just an old hat pin. Yet she treasured it because it had belonged to the mother of the love of her life, and he obviously valued it greatly.

Months went by without a word from him. Her anguish grew as time passed, but the faint hope of him showing up unexpectedly one day lived on in her heart. As those months turned to years, Mary's eccentricities began to show in unusual ways. She would go into crowded stores, and if someone bumped into her or pushed her out of their way, she would reciprocate with the sting of her beloved sailor's mother's hat pin, which she kept poised and at the ready, stuck in her black felt hat, just one action away from becoming a stinging experience for some unsuspecting victim.

After inheriting a substantial fortune from her spinster aunt, Hat Pin Mary then began to frequent sporting events, her favorite being professional wrestling matches. She became a celebrity because the local TV station (Channel Five) commentators would point the camera at her and her antics as part of their broadcasts. Hat Pin Mary became an early-era local TV celebrity without being totally aware of it. As with Iron Jaw Joe, she was considered a Red Hook superstar. But neither ever fully realized the extent of their celebrity.

Why, Joe had actually been a guest on Groucho Marx's *You Bet Your Life* TV show, where he had responded to one of Groucho's questions regarding where Omaha was located. Joe didn't know the answer, and when Groucho told him it was in Nebraska, he asked, "Which-a country is that in, Mister Groucho?" That question brought down the show's Golden Goose award and solidified Iron Jaw Joe's place in the Red Hook Mensa Society's hall of fame.

But getting back to Hat Pin Mary, though she looked much older than her years, she moved like a much younger person. Her garb and messy, gray hair did not complement her looks in any way. She was about average height and slender in body type. She seldom talked much, with the exception of responding to questions about her favorite sports.

Mary Maguire, who had gone to school with her at Public School (PS) 30, felt sorry for her and tried to befriend her by inviting her to go to bingo with John and her. The first time she took them up on it was the last time Mary invited her. They went to the bingo game held at Visitation Catholic Church hall in the neighborhood, located on Verona Street just across from Coffey Park.

As they set themselves at their bingo hall table, Mary and John spread out their game cards and got ready for the first number to be called. Old Hat Pin wasn't sure how to do that but was helped by John as he pointed out the specifics of the game. She shook her head as if she understood his instructions, but she didn't understand a word of what he had said.

At the end of the first game, several people in the parlor yelled, "Bingo!" simultaneously and waved their hands in celebration. "What just happened, John?" she mumbled, not understanding that those people had just won the first game of the night.

He leaned toward Hat Pin, not hearing all of what she had said. He took a guess at what she meant and responded quietly. "They just won the first round. That's what we need to be doing with the next round."

Hat Pin put her hand to her ear to hear him better. "Next round of what? A drink? You buying, John? If you're buying, then I'm sure as all hell drinking."

Buying her a drink was the last thing John would have suggested even in his wildest moments, for that lady was known to have cleaned out even the toughest of neighborhood saloons with simply the wielding of her notorious hat pin. After having had just a few belts of whiskey, the woman was unstoppable.

The second game was called and won on the twelfth number. Hat Pin asked, "What happened this time, John?"

"Another one we didn't win, Mary," he commented while shuffling his cards, shaking his head. His wife, Mary, did the same, trying to change her luck by repositioning all of her eight bingo cards. She ran a finger through a side curl in her dark hair as she stared, deep in thought, at the card alignment before her. Then she rearranged them all again.

"I think this is fixed!" Hat Pin grumbled as she moved around in her seat. John hoped that she would win a game and settle down. She peered around the hall, looking for perceived cheaters, and her glance came to rest on Mrs. Gallagher, who was calling the bingo game numbers while seated at a big table in the front of the hall. "I think I know where the fix is." She pointed toward the front. "I'm keeping an eye out." She looked intently toward the unsuspecting and kindly Mrs. Gallagher, who so generously volunteered her time at the church for such things as calling bingo games.

"Why are you pointing at Mrs. Gallagher?" Mary Maguire asked with some concern.

"I think she may be favoring her friends, and that would not be fair. Or even right." She squinted as she responded. That was not always a good sign when dealing with Hat Pin Mary.

John said, "Mary, we are with honest people here. No one's trying to fix this game. They couldn't even if they tried." He smiled as he tried to settle the old girl down by reassuring her that there was no cheating going on in the Visitation bingo hall that night.

"Okay, John. If you say so. But I'm keeping an eye out just the same." She put her attention back on the three cards she had lying in front of her. "I think I'll move these babies around too." She set about moving them, but they wound up back exactly where they were when she began.

"B-five," came the first number called in the third game.

"Now that's more like it." Hat Pin Mary had that number and was now totally focused on the card because of it. She looked up at Mrs. Gallagher as she was calling the next number, which Mary also had. That perked up the old warrior, and now she was fully engaged, waiting for the next number. It was not one of hers. Nor was the next.

Then came the third number, and it belonged to Hat Pin Mary. She shuffled in her seat as she looked fiercely at the large bingo board in the front of the hall. It was right behind where Mrs. Gallagher, happily smiling, was sitting while she called the game.

"There ought to be someone to complain to if there's any shenanigans here," Hat Pin Mary grumbled as she pointed toward the front of the hall.

Just then, Teresa Galucci, wife of the don and a hefty woman, made her way to the table John and the two Marys were occupying. "Do you have . . . ?" Her voice trailed off as she aborted her question about room for her and her friend Tina, another somewhat obese older lady. Mrs. Galucci looked at Mary Maguire and asked sternly, "What's she doing here?" She pointed to Hat Pin Mary.

"What do you mean?" John answered, his annoyance a bit pronounced in his tone.

"You know what I mean, John," she spat back.

"Eh, if I were you, I wouldn't do that." John let out a breath of caution as he spoke, thinking about the disaster that could be just a hair's length away if Hat Pin Mary were provoked.

"Why not?" Teresa Galucci laughed insultingly and turned and left the table, waddling closer to the front of the hall, where she joined several other women who greeted her warmly.

"That woman!" Mary Maguire said while trying to not set Hat Pin off any further. She was trying to demonstrate her support for Hat Pin Mary and her right to play bingo at the Visitation hall. The candy lady sitting at an adjoining table, who overheard the conversation, stated, "She can be such a bitch . . . that one."

Mrs. Gallagher called three more numbers, and someone at the Galucci table yelled, "Bingo!" The people at that table were all smiling and congratulating Teresa Galucci as she stood up and took a mock victory bow.

"How the hell did that just happen?" John asked, expressing his dismay at Teresa Galucci's win after playing through only half a game.

"See, I told ya." Hat Pin Mary started to stand up as John tried to settle her down, hoping she wouldn't get into it with either Mrs. Gallagher or Mama Teresa Galucci.

The rest of the evening went by almost without incident as Hat Pin Mary won a big jackpot and Mary and John won a small one. As the night ended and they were filing out of Visitation's hall, Teresa Galucci made the mistake of bending over to pick up a dollar bill that someone had dropped. The hefty Teresa quickly bent down, then picked it up saying, "Hey, look-a what I just found." As she started to straighten up, she felt the sharp sting of a stealthily placed pin hit her right square in the butt. "Ouch!" she screamed, turning around to see if she could find who had stuck her. But she found no one who she could wave a finger at. Not even the stealthy Hat Pin Mary, who she expected to see. "Son of a bitch, that really hurt. If I get my hands on whoever did that, I'll slap them into tomorrow." She rubbed her rear.

Hat Pin Mary never had anyone who could attest to her "stick-ings" because she had that action down to a science, and there was no one who could prove it was her. Even though they all knew it was. Some of the ladies leaving there that night chuckled quietly as they enjoyed the sight of Teresa Galucci "getting hers."

SEVEN

Bringing in the Spring

It was approaching eight o'clock in the evening, and both John and Mary were tidying up the store as they prepared to close the door. They especially enjoyed this part of the day because it was then they could relax with some of the Mensa friends. Especially on this warm spring evening, sitting outside on the sidewalk in front of the store. Mary handed out the aluminum folding beach chairs to the group of seven, who waited for them patiently. They were unfolded and occupied immediately. The conversation for that evening began with Lulu talking about the upcoming Memorial Day parade, which was being planned by the Veterans of Foreign Wars Post.

"They are tryin' to get the Cath-o-lick school kids marchin' with us in their uniforms. They're always so cuuuuuute." She commented proudly as she pursed her face, "We're gonna have the Visitation Parish marching band, an' they've added a few more different instruments too." She shook her head as she spoke, emphasizing her belief in the importance of all this.

Mary asked, "Mr. Casey still leading the band?"

"He's got a new name . . . no, I mean they call him somethin' different now." Lulu presented her news as an insider, and she relished that perceived role.

John laughed quietly. "Casey's the 'leader of the band.' Get it?"

Sal responded immediately, "No! I don't get it."

"You know what I mean. Come on." John continued laughing because he thought he had made a funny.

Charlotte Hayes, a close friend of Mary Maguire, joined in the conversation as she shifted in her uncomfortable chair. "Casey was the one who was 'at bat' in that poem about him striking out on a ball team. Not the leader of the band." She pushed her salt-and-pepper hair off her forehead as she tried relaxing back into her chair. Lucky for her that she was a slight woman because if she were heavier, that chair would have been a lot less comfortable.

Connie, Sal's wife, jumped in with "Casey was the one in the song who 'danced with the strawberry blonde.' " Connie was a middle-aged woman who, as John would say, was "no bigger than a minute." (But she was as large as a tiger when challenged.)

"Okay, so I got the wrong song and poem, but Casey is the leader of this band. Right?" John commented with a bit of mock frustration.

"Yeah, that's-a right, John." Iron Jaw Joe rose to the defense of his friend John Maguire, and that's how the conversation went for that evening. The Mensas were in full session until around nine-thirty, when having solved all of the world's and neighborhood's problems, they adjourned and all started heading home. John put the chairs up and set the burglar alarm on the store before he and Mary started walking slowly home, enjoying the warm spring night in Red Hook, Brooklyn.

They ran into Billy the Bird as they crossed the close by Dykeman Street. "Hey, Johnny, would you ask Raymundo, the Puerto Rican, to call me tomorrow?"

John nodded yes and was handed a piece of paper with Billy's phone number scribbled across it. "Sure, Billy. I can do that. He's always the first one in for coffee in the morning. I'll give it to him then."

"Me an' Harold gotta talk with him about somethin' I hope he can help us with."

"Raymundo is a good man," Mary commented.

Billy dwelled on Mary's words. "You think he's okay to trust with something that could be really big? Like earthquake big?" He was looking to have his trust in Raymundo confirmed.

"I don't know how to answer that, Billy." John thought for a moment before he went on. "I guess it would depend on how much money was at stake." He looked at Billy, wondering where he was going with this. "They say that everyone has their price, ya know."

Mary said, "I think he can be trusted and, Johnny, you don't have a price. At least not one that I've heard in all our years together."

"You'd be surprised." He made a face as he made a feigned ducking action, as if his wife were taking a poke at him. "Give me winning horse and I'm all yours." He laughed.

"That's your price?" Mary put her hands on her hips and continued good-naturedly, "Johnny, you're saying that's your price?"

"Nah . . . No one's ever even come close to my 'price,' my darlin'." He put his arm around his wife and pulled her closer to him.

"Yeah. I bet." She liked hearing his words despite that comment.

"See ya tomorrow," Billy said as he hurried off.

They continued on their slow walk home, enjoying their conversation and each other's company.

It was not quite six the next morning when Mary rolled the shades up on the front door of the Maguire's Brooklyn candy store. The day began with Raymundo's coffee and his daily pack of L&M cigarettes, with the addition of Billy the Bird's phone number and request for him to call.

"What's this about, Yohnny?" Raymundo had trouble with pronouncing his "J"s.

"I don't know, Ray. But Billy's a good kid with a lot of big ideas. Maybe this is about one of them. He asked me to ask you to call him. It sounded like it was important. That's all I know."

"Hmmm," was Raymundo's only response as he pocketed the number and grabbed his coffee and cigarettes before heading out the door.

The next customer was Carl or "Shackles the Cop," as he was known in the neighborhood. He was on early shift this week, walking the Van Brunt Street beat with his night stick and his eye for the ladies. At age thirty-five, he had reached his level of competency as a cop and was now settled into the fact that for the rest of his law-enforcement career, he would be pounding a beat in Brooklyn. Carl was about five-ten in height and a little over two hundred pounds with a round face, dark hair, and a pencil-thin mustache.

"Mary, Mary, Mary," he said in greeting as he entered the store.

She acknowledged this with a smile and a nod of her head. "John, John, John."

He looked at John, who was busy behind the counter with his usual morning job of making coffee. He respected both of them a great deal and looked forward to his coffee breaks in their store.

"Carl, Carl, Carl," John replied, completing the morning verbal ritual they shared every day that Carl was patrolling the Hook.

Shackles knew everybody on his beat and also what they were up to. The neighborhood had a bad reputation everywhere except in the actual neighborhood. People from outside of Red Hook feared anyone who came from there, thinking that anyone who could survive living there had to be "as bad as they come." Actually, it wasn't as tough a place as its reputation portrayed, but those who dwelled within liked having the rest of the borough and the city think it was. It gave them an edge when dealing with outsiders.

He ordered his usual: a cup of coffee and an onion roll as he slid up onto one of the eight stools at the counter. Resting his night stick on the stool next to him, he looked around the store and smiled. "This place always feels so clean every time I come in," he complimented. "Jimmy, Jimmy, Jimmy," he uttered as the owner of the fruit store ambled in for his morning brew.

"Carl, Carl, Carl," came his pleasant response. He liked Carl and having him on the beat gave Jimmy comfort, especially now that old Moose Miller was gone. Coffee in hand, Jimmy smiled at everyone as he went toward the door. "See you, see you, see you all later." He was in a hurry to get his store ready for the day's customers.

Speaking in threes or echoes happened only when Carl was in the store, for some strange reason. However, it was picked up on by Tim Maguire, the oldest of the Maguire children, and he used it to name his band "The Echoes." And when he turned twenty-one, his band had a Top 10 hit record. They appeared on the *Dick Clark Bandstand Show*, and he told that story when they were asked how they came up with the name of the group.

Carl asked, "How's that crazy son of a bitch Harold doing lately, John?"

"Same as always. Gets a little bit crazier with each passing day, it seems."

"He had me pissing my pants one day when he runs up to me with his tape measure and starts to measure me from head to toe." He laughed before continuing his story. "He says, 'Hey, Shackles, I got just the box for you when it comes your time. I'll make ya a great deal.' So I says, 'How do you do that when I'm already dead?' Then he says, 'Doesn't matter. I'll take it out your pockets. Not one cent more than what it costs. You know that, Carl!'

"'What happens with the rest of the money?' I asks. He comes back with 'What do you want me to do with it?' Now that is one funny undertaker. Of all the people in the world, who would believe that an undertaker would be the funniest one you'd meet in this life? So I tell him to give it to you, John, so you can play a winning horse."

"Give it to me? Shit, Carl, the horses I play have to have search parties go out looking for them after the winners cross the finish line."

Mary said, "It's not only that he's funny but he is also really smart."

"Yeah, he not only went to college but he even graduated." John was always admiring of those who went to college. An opportunity never presented to him in life.

"Hey, Carl . . . it's good ta see ya!" Billy the Bird came through the door, smiling broadly at the neighborhood beat cop he had come to like despite getting whacked on his ass by Carl's deadly accurate night stick. But that was back in the days when Billy was acting like a punk kid, urged on by his other punk kid friends in the struggle against "the Man." It took a while before Billy and his friends came to realize that it was actually Carl who kept things sane and reasonable on those particular streets of Brooklyn.

"Billy, Billy, Billy," came Carl's greeting, without him looking up from his coffee and onion roll.

"Good ta see ya. Good ta see ya . Good ta see ya." Billy caught up with the vocal cadence as he slid onto the stool next to Shackles.

"How are your birds doing, Billy?" The round-faced cop chuckled as he spoke, knowing full well the whole story about Billy's misadventure with his homing pigeons. "What are ya feeding them these days?"

"I know that there ain't nothin' I could say right now that would really explain how big a screw-up that all was . . . without getting myself locked up, that is." He sat looking at himself in the mirror that covered the wall behind the counter. He pumped up the pompadour wave that sat on the front of his head and halfway down his forehead. Turning to Carl, he asked, "You know anything about metal?"

The officer scrunched his face in mild confusion. "I know nothin' about metal. Why would you think I do?" He seemed surprised by Billy's inquiry.

"Uh, uh . . . I . . . I'm trying to find someone who knows some-thin' about metal and can give me some advice." Billy twisted to and fro on his stool as he spoke.

"Yeah, I can understand that, Billy, but why would you think that I know anything about metal?" He seemed a bit disturbed with discussing what he might know about metal.

"I don't mean nothin' by that, Carl. I just thought that with you being an officer of the law, you might have some ideas about metal. That's all."

"Nah . . . I don't have anything to say about it because I don't know anything about springs."

Billy and John made note of the fact that Billy hadn't mentioned anything at all about a spring. Billy's question was about metal. What they did not know was that Fat Pat had been talking with Shackles about Harold's and Billy's spring and offered him a "taste" of what-ever they could make on it.

Carl took a deep breath before he said, "I gotta tell ya, kid, you need to be on your toes and keep your eyes open. That includes that crazy bastard you're hooked up with on your little enterprise here. You understand?"

"Not sure," Billy responded.

"Well, let me put it like this. There are those who want to rip you guys off with something they shouldn't even know that you have."

"The spring?" the Bird asked, feeling concern rising up his spine.

"The spring," Carl repeated.

"What should we do with this?"

"Like I said, keep your eyes open and be careful who you trust. If this thing is as big as I'm hearing it is . . . somebody's gonna make some money . . . maybe big money. That draws assholes to it like sharks are drawn to blood."

"So if somebody steals it, can I count on you to do something?" Billy needed to hear something good at that moment.

"What can a simple beat cop like me do with this, Billy? What you need, and I think you need this right away, is a lawyer. Get yourself a lawyer who you can trust and who knows what to do with inventions."

"Yeah, that's good, Carl. That's good. But I don't know no lawyers like that. Do you?"

Carl shook his head no.

Carmine, the numbers guy, came through the door and patted Carl on the back as he greeted him with "Carl, Carl, Carl. How are you today?"

"Carmine, Carmine, Carmine, I'm feeling good. And how are you?"

"Couldn't be better." He said hello to everyone else in the store as he eyed John, looking for his "number," the three-number combination that everyone in the neighborhood bet on just about every day in their quest for riches.

"Put me down for three-three-three today, Carmine." Carl pulled a dollar out his pocket and handed it to the bookie.

John offered, "I'll take three sevens." He gave Carmine two bucks, one for him and one for Mary.

"I want, eh, four-fourteen." It was the number that Al, 'the Filipino,' always bet, but he was out of town for the week, so Mary spoke for him.

Carmine ordered a cup of coffee and took it with him as he made his rounds.

Carl put his hat back on and stood up as he prepared to leave. He asked Billy, "Can you guys put together a device I can use on my night stick?"

"Why would you want that? I never heard about you hitting anybody with that stick." Billy laughed.

"That's the magic, kid. No one has ever seen me do it. Keeps the complaints down. So what about it? A spring for my stick." He was serious about it.

"I'll check with Harold," Billy said as Carl left the store.

EIGHT

Ghost Bird

Olympia Cafiero was a member of the Red Hook Mensa Society, even though she didn't make as many meetings as most of the others who gathered so faithfully at John and Mary's. Standing almost six feet tall, with her thick body, she could be an imposing figure—especially in the dark. A woman from Italy, or "the other side," as it was often referred to, she spoke English with a dominating Italian accent.

Her pride and joy was a parrot whom she had named Sylvio. He was prolific with his bilingual ability of Italian and English and did not enjoy being disturbed by anything other than having his water bowl filled and his seed dish replenished. He had very limited flight capability and made a lot of noise when he half flew around the Cafiero apartment. Sylvio enjoyed sitting in his cage on the fire escape during the warm spring and summer days of coastal Brooklyn, where he could catch the natural flow of moist air and flap his wings on his perch every now and then.

"Billy, atsa so nice a' you to a-take a-care of my Sylvio so Vito an-a me can a-go back to Italia for-a to see my brother, who is a-no feeling good," Olympia greeted Billy after he slowly opened his door.

He smiled broadly at Olympia, who was holding the cage, then smiled at Vito, her husband, who was holding a bag of bird food. Vito was a few inches shorter than his wife. They were both in their mid-fifties, and Vito's bushy mustache covered half his plump face and matched the salt-and-pepper color of his thick, curly hair.

"Come in. Come in," Billy greeted them warmly. He loved having the opportunity to spend some time with the spirited Sylvio, who at times seemed to actually be able to carry on a conversation like a person. And there were those who were friends with the Cafieros, who could attest to being around Olympia when such conversations actually did occur.

The Cafieros visited for a short time and then were on their way. Vito said, "Billy, if a-Sylvio is a-no behave, then you shoulda put the cover on-a his cage. That will-a piss him off but a-will make-a him behave. You gotta that? I'm a-gonna give-a you a-somethin' good when I get back for taking a-care of that crazy son of a bitch."

"Yeah, I got that," Billy said, reassuring Vito that he could handle the bird.

No sooner was the door closed behind them when Sylvio screeched quite clearly, "Olympia, you son of a bitch, come back-a here."

Billy broke into a hearty laugh, which caused Sylvio to flap his green, feathered wings and again screech, "Olympia. You son of a bitch. Come back-a here." He fluttered around the cage, having a parrot temper tantrum. "Olympia, you son of a bitch, come back-a here." Sylvio closed one of his eyes whenever he spoke, looking like a pirate parrot, making his appearance even funnier than what he was saying.

Billy's mother Janet came home during one of Sylvio's rants, and before she could see that it was a bird talking, she said, "I think you'd better tell your friend to quiet down a little. Somebody'll think there's a murder being committed here." She put her bag of groceries down on the kitchen table before walking into the living room and spotting Sylvio. She then fell into a hearty laugh, realizing where the words were coming from. "It's that crazy Olympia's bird!" She continued laughing, pointing at the cage, her other hand covering her mouth.

"Awk, *faccia brutta*," came Sylvio's comment as he turned his back on her. And to make his point, promptly let go a dropping directly on the newspaper on the bottom of the cage.

"I guess he told you what he thinks of you." Billy laughed.

"Why, that little son of a bitch," came his mother's reply. "He called me ugly in Italian."

"That's his first language. What'd ya think, Ma?" Billy was really getting a kick out this feisty bird's antics and his mother's interaction with him.

"I think he'd better watch his mouth because when your father gets home, he ain't gonna put up with no squawking parrot insulting me. Ya hear me, Billy? Ain't gonna happen, my boy." In a minor huff, she busied herself putting away the groceries.

"Relax, Ma. We can have a lot of fun with this guy here. I'm telling ya. Right, Sylvio?"

Billy picked the cage up, put it in his room, and placed the cover over it. Sylvio was not happy, and he squawked for a minute or two. "Hey, Scootch, what-a you do?" Then went on with "You better a-stop that!" The voice was like a precise recording of the person Sylvio mimicked perfectly, repeating what he had heard at one time or another by one Vito Cafiero.

"Time to take a nap now, Sylvio, my little buddy."

"*Aspetto!*" came the screech of the unhappy bird, telling Billy to "wait" in his first language. But Billy was not taking orders from a parrot, at least not that day.

"Go to sleep, little buddy," Billy said as he closed the door to his room behind him, hoping it would quiet the flustered bird down for a while. Before he left the room, an idea popped into his head. What if he suspended the cage from the ceiling, attached to the latest version of Harold's spring? "I wonder what would happen when Sylvio goes into his tantrum dance? Yeah, I wonder what would happen?" A slight smile appeared on his face as he headed out the door on his way to Stadermann's hardware store, two blocks away.

"You want what, Billy?" Old Man Stadermann asked, trying his best to get Billy's order done right.

"I need a hook so I can hang something from my ceiling," Billy explained.

"What something is that, son?" The kindly old store owner asked.

"A bird cage."

"How big is it?"

Billy responded, "How big is what?"

"The cage!"

"Oh, I don't know. It's for a parrot."

"Oh, you mean Sylvio. You got him now?" Stadermann chuckled. "I was wondering when Olympia would throw him out. He's got such a foul mouth . . . that bird."

"He's funny. I get such a kick outta him." Billy grinned.

"You know that building the Cafieros live in has some strange things happen from time to time. So the way that bird behaves makes me wonder if it's something in the building making him that way."

"You know, you may be right on that, Mr. Stadermann. Because I knew a guy who lived there when Shoy's bakery was on the bottom floor. He had a big German shepherd named Blackie, and that dog was the greatest animal in the world until he was in the hallway of that building. He would just sit his ass down and refuse to move. Whimpering and even crying, like dogs do, when they're scared a' somethin'."

"Then you never heard the stories? That's what you're telling me, Billy?" Stadermann shook his head almost in disbelief.

"No. What stories? Go ahead, tell me." He was focused on what the hardware store owner was saying.

Mr. Stadermann took his glasses off and wiped them clean as he started telling the story. "This man, Milo—I think was his name— had a mother who was part deaf, so she talked a little louder than most people and that used to annoy Milo. He criticized her over and over again for doing it.

"So the old lady dies suddenly, and Milo and his wife are grieving an awful lot because Milo feels that he disrespected her, especially right before she died. He supposedly really got nasty with her, calling her names and all that mean stuff. So he really carried on, feeling awfully guilty. He was missing his mother so badly, he went around telling nearly everyone he came into contact with that he would give anything to hear her voice just 'one more time.' He even came in here once and bought something, but before the poor man left, he told me the story about what a bad guy he was for treating the old lady so disrespectful."

"It's funny, but I never heard about this. I never met this guy, Milo, neither. Could all this have happened when I was in the army?" Billy asked.

Stadermann shrugged his shoulders. "I don't know, Billy. Maybe it was during that time." He took a hook out of one of the small drawers in the supply counter that was immediately behind him. Laying it down, he pointed to it. "Is this what you're looking for?"

"Yeah, that's it, Mr. Stadermann, but what's the rest of the story with these people?"

"Oh yeah. So then, in the middle of the night, he wakes up and hears a voice calling out in the darkness, 'Milo, Milo.' He jumps up and must have lost control when he realized it was the voice of his dead mother. And from what I heard from people who lived in the building at the time, Milo and his wife ran screaming out of their apartment and down the stairs onto Van Brunt Street at three o'clock in the morning, screaming, "Ghost! Ghost!" They had the police show up and go through the apartment . . . and they found nothing."

"Nothing?" Billy asked, deeply engrossed in what he was hearing.

"Nothing."

"Now here's where this all gets really strange." Stadermann smiled as he leaned across the counter, propped up on his elbows. "Here's what really happened that night. Maybe this will make you feel better." The old man patted Billy on the shoulder. "Quite a while after Milo and his wife had run out of the neighborhood, Vito Cafiero heard the old lady's voice one night. He thought it was coming from outside his kitchen window, and it was. It was coming from Sylvio's cage."

"What?" Billy asked.

"After he got over thinking he had heard a ghost, Vito put together that what could have happened was what Milo had heard was the parrot mimicking his mother's voice. It could have happened that, since she talked so loud, he could hear her when he was in his cage on the fire escape, and the little son of a gun probably got into Milo's apartment one night through the always-open kitchen window and called him." Stadermann and Billy were both laughing heartily, bent over the counter.

"But how would he get out of his cage?" Billy thought out loud.

"I think it had a faulty latch. I know that because Vito came in here asking for a clip he could use to secure the cage, preventing Sylvio from getting out. If you put two and two together . . . " Stadermann shrugged.

"Man, this Sylvio is one character, huh?" Billy took the small hook from the counter and after saying so long to Mr. Stadermann, he hurried back home, hoping that he could get there before his father. He raced up the three flights of stairs and through the apartment door to his bedroom. Taking a stepladder out of the closet, he climbed up to a level where he could touch the ceiling. Tapping lightly, he found a stud and went about screwing the hook into the support beam above his head. When he got down and off the ladder, he searched his dresser drawers and found Harold's super spring. Stepping back onto the ladder, he attached it to the hook, followed by Sylvio's cage.

And the fun began anew as Sylvio started his tantrum dance, calling Olympia a son of a bitch several times. He hopped from his perch to the side of the cage and then back to the perch, causing the cage to bounce up and down and to and fro. And in walked Billy's father in the middle of the pandemonium caused by the tyrant parrot.

"What the hell is that?" was Tony Guarino's greeting as he rumbled through the door, holding his hands over his ears to save them from Sylvio's screeching, Billy's belly-laughing, and his wife Janet's screaming at Billy for bringing Sylvio into their home.

"That is a sign of your son's stupidity, Tony!" Janet said, pointing her finger rigidly at Billy. "He agreed to babysit that crazy bird for the time the Cafieros go back to the old country. For about two months, Tony! *For two friggin' months.*"

"What have you got to say for yourself, Billy?" asked Tony.

"What can I say, Dad?" Billy shrugged. "The bird will settle down. He ain't really so bad . . . He's even funny most a' the time. Come on."

"Come on . . . what? You got your mother so upset, she's gonna have agita all night now." He stared hard at his son. "And that ain't right."

Suddenly, Sylvio went absolutely silent. They all looked at one another, wondering what had happened but thankful for the quiet moment.

Billy pointed toward his bedroom, whispering, "Maybe he decided to shut up and take a nap. Let me go see." He walked quietly into his bedroom, laughing at what had just happened. When he came back out, he yelled, "He flew the coop. The little bastard's gone!"

"What? You didn't lock his cage?" Janet asked, somewhat surprised.

Billy freaked out and sprang into action, looking for the feisty bird as he climbed out his bedroom window and onto the fire escape, thinking that Sylvio had taken that route in his escape since there was no other way out of that room. He climbed down one flight to the second story, and since the kitchen window was open, he assumed that the bird was somewhere inside that apartment. No one seemed to be home, so Billy leaned through the windowsill and called, "Sylvio . . . Sylvio." He paused for a few moments before calling again. He heard nothing and thought about going through the window to have a look inside, but decided it best that he didn't. He called one more time, then went back up the fire escape and into his apartment.

"Find the bird?" his father asked gruffly.

"No."

"Good. Last thing I need is that squawking pain in the ass messing up my life."

"Come on, Pop. Where's your sense a' humor these days?" Billy asked. "It's just a freakin' bird."

"I got your sense a' humor right here," came the elder Guarino's caustic reply.

"I gotta find that bird. Olympia trusted me with him, and she don't trust nobody with that crazy animal." Billy's voice was laced with serious concern. "I can't figure out where he went." He shook his head in frustration. What he didn't realize was that the crafty bird had more flight in his wings than anyone, including the Cafieros, believed. Sylvio had landed in the backyard of the Guarino's apartment building and then made his way, hop-flying, over two fences to the yard behind John and Mary's candy store. He flew into their barred but opened window. He settled in for the night in the rear studio apartment that was part of John and Mary's store.

John was the first one into the store at six the next morning, beginning his daily ritual of turning on the coffee brewing machines and bringing in the stacks of newspapers, which were baled and lying on the steps outside the store. He threw them on top of the newspaper stand in the front of the store, right at the door. As he returned to the coffee machines, he thought he heard someone talking. It sounded like an old woman. A sudden thought ran through his head. His mother-in-law had died in the studio apartment in the rear of the store two years before, and now he thought that he was hearing a woman's voice saying, "You son of a bitch," which was how she had addressed him sometimes. Could it be her ghost talking?

"Holy shit, that sounds like the old lady," he said to himself as he stared into the darkness in the back of the store and the apartment behind it. The hair suddenly stood up on the back of his neck as he heard it again—this time more clearly. "You son of a bitch."

"Who's there?" He paused, waiting, then heard, "You son of a bitch, come back here."

"She's calling me to go back to where she is," he thought, uncharacteristically panicking. He turned and sprinted toward the door, faster than he had moved in the past twenty years. As he ripped through the doorway, he flattened his wife as she was entering. John didn't stop running until he hit the other side of Van Brunt Street. When he realized that his wife was lying totally winded and flat on her back on the sidewalk outside the store, he froze.

Gaining control of himself, he moved quickly back across the street to his wife's side and helped her to her feet. She was a bit dazed and angry. "Johnny, what the hell was that?"

"Your mother," he stammered.

"My mother?"

"Yeah, your mother." He held her hand as he spoke imploringly. "She's in the back of the store."

"You're talking crazy. You know she's been gone for a couple a' years now. What are you saying?"

"I just heard her calling to me to go to her. She was in the back of the store, in the apartment. I heard her clear as day," he said quickly.

"Why do you think it was her?"

"She called me a son of a bitch."

Mary thought for a moment. "Oh yeah, that could be her." Her mother had picked on John as she got cranky in her later years. She was a woman who liked her beer and would pester anyone around her for a "cold one." John tried to keep a lid on the amount she would consume, for her own good. She didn't see it that way, and thus, her references to him had often been a bit less than endearing.

"Let's go take a look back there." Mary started walking toward the apartment with John following closely behind. Sylvio, hearing the footsteps approaching, departed through the opened window just seconds before they entered.

Throwing the light switch on, they both stood in the doorway, surveilling the small space. Seeing nothing out of the ordinary, they moved slowly toward the bathroom. Thrusting the door open, they were both relieved to see it empty.

"I heard your mother calling me a son of a bitch, Mary. I know it sounds crazy, but that's what I heard," he said adamantly.

"I'm not saying you didn't hear something, Johnny, but maybe what you heard was coming from somebody's radio?"

He reiterated slowly, "I heard your mother calling me to come back here. The only thing she didn't say was "And bring me a beer when you do, you son of a bitch.""

"Oh stop that, you fool. So now you're telling me that you finally believe in ghosts?"

"I do now. I'm telling you . . . I heard something, and no amount of talking is going to convince me otherwise." He continued scanning the apartment. "I heard someone saying something from right here. Now there is no way that anyone could get through those bars on the window, and the door is locked and dead bolted. So how do you explain it?"

"I'm not trying to explain anything, my love. You know me and what I believe about ghosts."

"Yeah, but that's because you're Irish," he said smugly.

"Well, so are you." She chuckled as she hugged him close.

"Yeah, ain't that the truth?" He had to laugh at himself. "I guess you can count me in on this."

"It happens to all of us at some point, honey," Mary said confidently.

John asked, "Are you okay?" He studied her closely, hoping she wasn't injured from getting knocked down.

"You'll know the answer to that if I hit you over the head with a frying pan," she said lightly. After hearing Mary say that she was okay, John went back to work, preparing the store for the day. Sylvio continued his exploration of the apartment houses close to the candy store while Billy was on a desperate quest to find him. The chase continued.

NINE

The Paper Gangster

Pat Galucci sat in his Cadillac, talking with his underboss pal Junior Defonte as they surveilled Billy the Bird's tenement, watching for his comings and goings and those of his mother and father. He had been made aware of the fact that the kitchen window of their third-floor apartment remained open all the time during the warm weather months, and he and Junior were planning to make an unannounced and uninvited visit while no one was home. Pat was obsessed with getting his hands on the "super spring" and the experimental remote bed-opening device that he had heard Billy was on the verge of bringing into existence. A device that could "change the world for apartment dwellers everywhere!" (That was according to Pat Galucci.)

This was their second day of surveillance, and they believed that they had the Guarino's schedule all figured out. Pat mumbled, "We're gonna take a little ride just in case somebody's watching us . . . to throw them off." Before starting the engine, he pulled a comb from his pocket and used it on his thick mop of dark brown hair, which he kept subdued with a dab of Brylcreem. His face filled the rearview mirror, and when he finished combing, he had to readjust the view a bit. He nudged Junior with his right arm and said, "Ehh-hh?" as he smiled in self-admiration. "How do I look?"

"Gorgeous," came Junior's sarcastic response as he turned and looked out of the passenger-side window. He let out an annoyed breath.

"What are you, a joik . . . jerk?" Pat reacted to the sarcasm and corrected his Brooklynese pronunciation of the word.

"No, I mean it, boss. You look good . . . really good," he said, trying to recover from saying something he had actually believed originally.

Pat shot back, "Don't be a smart-ass. It don't suit you." He leaned into Junior menacingly in true bullying fashion, causing the under-boss to lean back away from him and press against the car door. "Get me?" Galucci pressed him. "Look, we're gonna take a ride up Richard Street to Coffey Park, then go back up to Van Brunt Street and head back this way."

"Why are you doing that?"

Pat relaxed and sat back into the driver's seat. Smiling, he tapped his forehead with his stout index finger. "I'm gonna really fool them."

Junior shrugged. "Who's them, Pat?"

"The assholes who are probably watching us," he stated emphatically.

Junior made a face. He didn't respond but thought, "Is this guy losing it? Who's watching us? The bulls? How would the cops know what we're doing here?" He watched Pat while wondering what was rolling around in his head.

As they drove along Richard Street, listening to the music on the radio, Pat was feeling good about the possibility of getting his hands on Billy's and Harold's invention. If he could pull that off, there was no limit to where he could go. He would be worth so much money that Frank Sinatra would be giving him private concerts. He daydreamed about his future lavish lifestyle where he would be surrounded by beautiful women and go-fers, all doing his bidding. His father would be at his beck and call, and his mother would be really happy in the fur coats and diamond rings he would lavish on her. Yes, sir, that would make him as important a person as anyone in New York City could have ever thought of being.

When they returned from their short ride, he parked in a different place a half of a block away. Pat said, "Let's go, Junior," as he lumbered out of the car and started walking toward Billy's apartment building. "We'll ring the bell in the hall first. Just to see if anyone answers. Make sure." He winked confidently. "Then we climb the stairs to the roof. And then we go to the fire escape and down the ladder to the Guarino's level, right below. And then, through the opened window, we're in!"

"Then what?"

"What are you, stupid? Then we go to work, finding the spring and the device which opens the fold-up couches automatically." Pat shrugged his shoulders as if asking, "What about this don't you understand?"

"Oh," came Junior's simple response.

"I don't know about you, Junior. Sometimes I think that you're just a little bit brain dead," Pat admonished.

"And sometimes I think you're an asshole," Junior thought in response, not about to say it out loud.

There was no response to the door bell ringing, so they slowly climbed the four flights of stairs to the roof. As they opened the roof door, they were greeted by the odor of pigeon droppings coming from the coop where Billy's birds resided.

"Smells pretty bad," Junior remarked as he made a face.

"No worse than your farts." Pat laughed in response.

"Or your breath?" Junior thought as they walked over to the ladder.

"You first." Pat pointed at the fire escape ladder, which was attached to the edge of the roof.

Junior shrugged. "Okay. Here goes." He climbed onto it and went down gingerly to the next level, which was the Guarino's, followed by Pat, who was quite awkward in his descent.

"In!" Pat grunted at Junior, as he pointed at the apartment's open window. And in the window his cohort went, followed by the clumsy wanna-be gangster. They moved slowly, side by side, through the apartment, scanning left and right as they went.

"What's this?" Pat asked as he picked up a can opener sitting on one of the kitchen counters.

"Looks like a can opener," Junior responded sarcastically.

"Of course it's a can opener, you jerk. But maybe it might be a little more than what it looks like?" Pat pontificated, acting like he knew more than he did.

"I don't follow you."

"Then follow this. The Bird is weird . . . but he is also slick. Why wouldn't he use something that he already has? Like this can opener." He looked the hand-sized utensil over closely, but seeing nothing more than what it was, he unceremoniously put it down, wishing he hadn't said anything about it in the first place.

Junior didn't say a word, knowing if he did, he would get an even dumber response.

"Holy shit! What's this?" Pat latched onto a spring lying on the coffee table in the living room. "Dis has gotta be it. Look, Junior." He examined it thoroughly, reaching the absolute conclusion that this was indeed the "magic" spring. "Who leaves springs laying out like this but a weird dick like the Bird?"

"Yeah, you're probably right, boss . . . But do you think he would leave it laying out in the open like this?"

"Sure he would. You know he wouldn't know that he'd be dealing with someone as smart as me," Pat crowed with a big smile as he poked Junior's arm playfully. "I got this all figured out. We're dealing with a couple a' assholes here. When all da dust is settled, they'll be wondering what happened, and we'll be in Hawaii with a couple a' hula-girls, drinking one a' them stupid pineapple drinks and counting our money." He chuckled. "You stick with me and you'll be going places."

"Places like where? Jail?" Junior worried to himself.

Pat slipped the spring into his pocket as he continued searching for the sleeper-couch opener. Just as he felt he was on the verge of locating it, his blood turned to ice as they both heard coming from one of the bedrooms the voice of a man shouting, "Olivia, you son of a bitch, come a-back here!"

"Holy shit!" Junior said as he ran to the door, followed closely by Pat tripping his way there as well. Swinging it open, they began to race down the stairs, Junior stumbling and Pat rolling down the last three steps to the second level. Getting up, they continued their rapid descent to the first floor and out the door to Van Brunt Street where they slowed to a walk so as to not call attention to themselves.

"Pat, who the hell was that?" Junior asked, really worried that they were in serious trouble for burglary.

"I don't know, but maybe he didn't see us, and we won't have anything to worry about. Just keep going to the car." Pat was breathing heavy as he gasped, "We're okay. We don't need to be freakin' out over this." He looked back over his shoulder to make sure no one was following them.

As they got into the car and began to drive away, heading for President Street, Sylvio made his way back out the Guarino kitchen window to the fire escape and down into the canyon-like yard, where he perched on a short tree, enjoying the warm Brooklyn sunshine. He looked at the fence that separated him from John and Mary's candy store and began to flap his wings, expecting to fly—but not more than several feet at a time.

Junior said, "It wasn't so smart that we didn't look in that bedroom when we got in that place."

"What d' ya mean? Ain't no way that we coulda known that there was someone in there. We rang the bell, right? Then there was no sound or anything that woulda let us know that there was someone there . . . Come on!"

"You think he was hiding? Who do you think it was?" Junior asked.

"Probably the old man," Pat ventured a guess.

"Billy's father?"

"Well, it didn't sound like the Bird. Did it?"

Little did either of them know that the Bird they were referring to was not the bird they had heard, and the device they were looking for had actually been lying right in front of them on the coffee table, in the form of the TV remote. Remotes in those days were about as basic a piece of equipment as anything.

"Ya know, I think that maybe the Irishman probably has the device in his laboratory. Probably hides it under the stiffs," Junior said, half lost in thought.

"For the first time in a long time, Junior, I think you finally said something that makes sense." Pat smiled broadly as he shook his head in the positive. "Maybe we need to give that asshole another visit. What d' ya think, eh?"

"I don't know, boss. That place gives me the friggin' creeps."

"Hey, don't be a bozo. You didn't get hit by a dead body . . . I did. An' I ain't afraid to go back there." Pat nudged his underling. "We're gonna do what we gotta do."

"Okay, but I ain't spending no time in that funeral parlor in the dark, like the last time," Junior stated emphatically.

"You're gonna do what I tell ya ta do. You got that, Junior?" Pat leaned into his face as he spoke, using his best intimidation expression.

Junior acquiesced but did not feel good about the prospect of a return to Harold's funeral parlor.

TEN

"That Friggin' Bird"

Sylvio returned to his cage perch on the Guarino fire escape with great fanfare as he screeched into the apartment, announcing his return. The senior Guarino yelled at his son, "I'm telling you, Billy . . . You gotta do something with that son of a bitching bird. Get him in his cage and take him the hell outta here."

He was adamant, and Billy knew he had to do something with the feisty creature. He understood why his mother and father were beside themselves due to the bird's loud screeching, and he knew that Sylvio had to be relocated before Billy found himself "relocated." He thought for a moment and then picked up the phone.

"Harold, I need a favor." He paused for a response from the undertaker and, getting none, he went on with, "I've been babysitting a parrot for a couple a' days, and now my father is telling me to get him outta our apartment. So I'm wondering if I can put him over at your parlor for a couple a' days or so."

"Does this bird, uh, shit all over the place, Billy?" Harold asked, chuckling a bit as he envisioned massive droppings all over the viewing room and maybe even on a corpse. Ironically, he saw that possibility as something hysterical.

"No, man. Of course not. He'll be in a cage the whole time he's there."

Harold slowed his laughing down to a mild chuckle as he played with Billy, knowing full well what a vulnerable situation Billy had placed himself in.

"Come on, Harold. Ya gotta help me out here."

"Does this bird communicate in the English language?" Harold was overtly enjoying the conversation and gaining leverage as it progressed.

"Of course he does." Billy's agitation was beginning to show in his tone. "But he can speak Italian if he's pissed off enough to do that."

"Does he . . . have an accent?" Harold was calmly riding his embattled partner.

"What kinda shit is that, Harold?"

"I'm just trying to break your balls a bit, Billy. Come on . . . bring the friggin' bird here. Ya gotta have a sense of humor, kid."

Billy was swept with relief at Harold's response. He walked Sylvio through the streets of Red Hook with the feisty bird sitting perched in his cage. He did not make a sound during the four-block trek.

Harold greeted Billy and bird with an impish grin as they entered his funeral parlor. "Put that crazy little bastard on that table right over there, in the corner." Harold pointed to the corner of the room, near his desk.

Sylvio regarded Harold, looking at him up and down, head to toe. He maintained his unusual silence but moved from side to side on his perch, dancing, as caged birds often do, for attention.

"He's awfully green, Billy." Harold commented as he bent down, hands on his knees, looking perch-level at Sylvio, eye to eye. "I've heard that Olympia argues with this little guy . . . and loses most of the arguments."

"Where'd you hear that? I didn't know you knew Olympia." Billy was somewhat surprised.

"I hear things, Billy." Harold grinned, wiggling his fingers, mimicking a magician. "You forget that everybody in this neighborhood passes through here on their way out. Their families talk. They talk about everybody and everything. As I said . . . I hear things." The Friendly Undertaker winked as he spoke, a twinkle shining in his eyes.

"I brought his food and this here water thing. I'll set it up for you," Billy said quickly, appreciating Harold's generosity. So much so that he would have shined his shoes to demonstrate his deep gratitude.

"How long will he be my guest?" Harold asked as he continued to study the now perch-pacing bird.

"I gotta be honest with you, Harold, this can be more than two days. Olympia and Vito won't be back for two months. They went to Italy, and the little bastard has really got my old man pissed. I'm afraid he might hurt him."

"So I could be stuck with him for two months?" Harold faked anger before he laughed. "Let's see how we get along. Okay?"

A greatly relieved Billy and a smiling Harold talked a bit about their project, and Billy explained the triggering device he had finally gotten in place in a converted TV remote. What remained was to get a radio receiver embedded in the spring to activate the opening and closing action on the sleeper sofa.

"We're gonna be rich, Harold. This is gonna put us on the map," Billy said assumingly.

"Your lips to God's ears, Billy." Harold's eyes shone as he grinned impishly. "Your lips to God's ears," he repeated slowly, truly savoring the idea of the potential in their invention.

"We gotta be really careful about Galucci and his shit," Billy suggested.

"What's with that fat bastard?"

"He's got his father interested in what we got, and the don has been pressuring me about it. Pat is diving into it with both hands . . . an' I know where that's going."

"I'm aware, Billy. Let us not forget that I had the grand pleasure of scaring the living shit out of him . . . and that nitwit sidekick of his, Junior." Harold laughed as he settled into his desk chair, his flushed Irish face beaming from the memory. "I can still see them charging up the street after old man Miller rose up in his casket and clocked that smart ass son of a bitch Pat right in the face. I wanted so bad to call out, 'Take that, you fat bastard!' " Harold laughed heartily.

"You shoulda done that," Billy affirmed.

"Done what?"

"Yelled out, 'Take that, you fat bastard!' " Billy was now laughing.

"Yeah . . . but I think it worked better the way it was. I wish I had a movie camera on him, though." The undertaker shook his head as he chuckled.

Billy had bent over as he belly-laughed with the image of the two running up the street dancing through his head. Sylvio shifted back and forth on his perch, mildly squawking, seemingly annoyed by the laughter.

When Billy left, Harold tried to get Sylvio to speak, but the bird remained unusually silent and just glared at him.

Billy stopped by John and Mary's for a cup of coffee. "What's been going on, guys?" he asked both of the storekeepers.

"Not much," John responded. "How 'bout you, Billy?"

"I just been doing some stuff that I hope is gonna pay big dividends."

"You talking about the ponies?" John perked up, hoping Billy might have a tip on a horse he could bet on.

"No . . . nothin' like that, John. Just a thing I've been working on with Harold. You know me . . . " He poured some cream in the dark, hot brew sitting before him and watched as it swirled on its own, reminding him of clouds and the way they moved.

Mary asked, "Billy, how are your mother and father doing? Haven't seen them for a few days. Are they okay?"

"Yeah, sure, they're all right. Maybe they got a little agita with me though." He kept his head down as he spoke in a regretful tone. "I did Olympia and Vito a favor, and it kinda blew up into a big family argument." He shrugged his shoulders as he raised the coffee to his mouth. He muttered quietly, "Sometimes things don't go the way you see them in your head . . . ya know?"

"Happens a lot, kid," John commented as he went about making more coffee. "That's what seems to always happen to me with the ponies." He chuckled.

"What happened, Billy?" Mary asked, a little bit concerned for him.

"Aw, it was that I did Olympia and Vito a favor by—"

Mary interjected. "By babysitting their crazy bird Sylvio . . . right?"

"Yeah . . . sorta . . . yeah." He shook his head regretfully.

"That little son of a bitch bird can be mean and crafty too," muttered John.

Mary chuckled. "I gotta tell you this, Billy. You see that man?" She pointed at her husband. "Well, Olympia conned us into bird-sitting him for a few days . . . an' listen to this." Mary went behind the counter over to John. "Johnny here decides to let the 'green monster' sit on his shoulder as he worked behind the counter, and before you could blink, that bird hops onto his head and sits there." She nudged John before continuing. "Then Iron Jaw Joe pops into the store and sees the bird sitting on John's head. He lets out a yell, coming straight for Sylvio . . . that little green son of a bitch lets out a loud screech and craps all over John's gray head." She doubled over, laughing at the memory. John didn't crack a smile as Billy spit the coffee onto the counter, laughing uncontrollably, picturing John trying to get the green monster off his head and keep the crap from flowing down his face.

––––––––

As the sun began to set, Harold began closing the funeral parlor early since there were no viewings scheduled for that evening. He made the mistake of opening the birdcage door and inviting Sylvio to jump onto his extended right arm.

The bird looked him up and down and then hopped on. He walked up Harold's arm, stopping at his shoulder, bit him on the ear and then flew off as the Friendly Undertaker swatted at him, reacting. What followed was a series of events that included Sylvio flying up to an exposed beam and sitting there as Harold stood on a chair, trying to coach the belligerent bird back onto his extended forearm. The agitated bird would have nothing to do with that and instead flew along the exposed rafters of the parlor to a high point where he hid. No amount of Harold's coaxing could get him to return to his cage or Harold's still-extended arm.

"Sylvio. You need to get your ass back here," Harold admonished without success. Sylvio had found a perch for the night and looked like he was not moving from there.

After a half hour of trying to coax the bird back into the cage, Harold gave up and decided to leave him be until morning. He closed the cage door so Sylvio could not get at his water and food, possibly making him more agreeable to return for them in the morning. Harold turned off the lights and closed up for the night. "Good night, you crazy little bastard," were his parting words.

"You fat bastard," came Sylvio's words as clear as a bell, causing Harold to get quite a laugh.

"He sounds just like a friggin' person," Harold thought as he closed the funeral parlor door for the night. "I gotta get me one of those," he mumbled to himself, thinking he could sure have some fun with people who visited his parlor with a bird like Sylvio. "You know, cheer them up during sad moments."

It was a little before midnight when Pat and Junior rolled slowly up King Street and parked close to the corner. They waited for Bruno, known in shadier circles as "the Locksmith," to get there so they could gain entry without having to force their way through the door and give away the fact that someone had broken in. Who breaks into funeral parlors anyway? Especially during the night.

A few minutes later, Bruno tapped on the driver's-side window, causing Pat and Junior to jump. They had both dozed off. "It's done. I left it unlocked. That's a real creepy place to be in the dark."

"You see any ghosts, Bruno?" Junior laughed.

"No, but it sure felt weird. As soon as I got the door unlocked and opened it a little, I could swear that I heard somebody say something." Bruno was a man in his early fifties, olive-skinned, short in stature, and in good shape for his age. He had done time in upstate Clinton Prison, right on the Canadian border, for burglary. He was the Galucci family go-to guy for "dark entries." One of the top safe crackers in Brooklyn as well.

Pat thanked him and told him he'd "tighten him up" the next day with some cash. He left as quietly as he had come.

Pat and Junior walked quickly to the funeral parlor halfway down the block. They looked around for any people in the street. Seeing none, and no one looking out their windows, they entered cautiously.

"Where do you wanna start, boss?" Junior asked as he looked around, feeling uncomfortable.

"Let's start by looking up at the ceiling." Pat had an exasperated look on his face. "What a friggin' stupid question." He shook his head at his underling before continuing with "Let's get started with his friggin' office first. Come on, follow me."

They inched through the dark lobby toward Harold's glass office door. Gingerly, Junior opened it and peered into the room, hoping to not see anyone. He breathed a sigh of relief because the office was empty. Pat shoved him in, and he stumbled and almost fell. Junior complained, "Hey, watch out. I coulda broke something here." He pulled at his belt as he spoke.

"Stop your bitchin'. We gotta move fast here, and I gotta think clearly without distractions from you. You take the desk, and I'll look in the closet," Pat ordered.

"What are we supposed to be lookin' for?" Junior asked as he started opening desk drawers.

"We're *supposed* to be lookin' for somethin' what looks like a spring," Pat said slowly, sarcasm dripping from his voice. "That's sorta why we're here in this friggin' mausoleum. Ain't it, Junior?"

"Yeah, I guess."

"Yeah, I guess," Pat mimicked with the sarcasm still in his voice.

They found nothing. "Let's go downstairs to where he lays out the stiffs. That may be where he does his experiments." Pat pointed in the direction of the stairs, which led down to the embalming room. "I'll bet that crazy Mick keeps everything down there. He's got a sick mind, Junior."

"Why do you say that, Pat? He's only goofy crazy. Not really crazy."

"He drains blood outta people for a livin'. That's what I consider sick." Pat stated with authority. But despite his pomposity, he, and Junior, missed the birdcage sitting right out in the open.

They inched their way downstairs to the embalming area and then searched the entire room. They finally found a mold in the shape of a spring on a shelf near a closet door. Then they found a small oven on another shelf below it.

"Looks like we're getting somewhere here," Pat proclaimed proudly.

"Uh, what do you call this?" Junior crowed as he held up a spring about a foot long and four or so inches in diameter. "Eh?" He was glowing, feeling pretty good about himself at that moment.

"Son of a bitch, Junior, you finally did somethin' right. Yeah." Pat threw his arm around his cohort. "We got it. We got the magic spring. Holy crap."

"Okay, now let's get outta here," Junior suggested strongly.

"No, let's see if there's anything else that might be of help to us," Pat said, surveilling the room some more. "Keep looking."

"Looking for what, Pat?" Junior was getting frustrated.

"For something that looks unusual."

"Like you?" Junior quipped.

"Keep it up, and I'll hit you so hard in that face a' yours that you will look unusual. Really unusual. Keep poking around here."

"Listen," Junior said, startled by a noise. "You hear that?" He pointed up towards the lobby.

"I didn't hear . . . " Pat's words trailed off as he heard the voice too. "Holy shit, we're gonna get made. Quick! Quick! Hide!" They started scrambling around the room until they found a closet, into which they both crammed themselves nose to nose, afraid to breathe.

"You think it's the bulls?" Junior asked squeamishly.

"Who the hell knows. We gotta keep quiet."

Minutes passed without another sound. Pat whispered, "I think maybe whoever it was maybe coulda left." They remained in the closet for a few more minutes, listening intently, but there was only silence.

"Let's go. But be quiet. We can't get caught here. That will blow this whole thing sky high."

They started moving slowly in the darkness, feeling their way forward toward the staircase. Pat held his breath, hoping he didn't come face-to-face with a cop. Junior held his breath, hoping he wouldn't come face-to-face with the ghost of Moose Miller.

They inched up the stairs, pausing every few steps to listen for any sound of activity in the building. Hearing none, they continued their climb. Pat signaled Junior to open the door back into the lobby. Swinging it slowly open, Junior tensed, closing his eyes in anticipation of someone putting the arm on them. When nothing happened, he let his pent-up breath loose.

"Let's just keep looking a little bit more," Pat whispered.

"I think we need to get outta this freakin' place," Junior strongly suggested.

"You don't get paid to think. Just clam up and keep looking," Pat ordered.

"I ain't got no idea what I'm supposed to be looking for," Junior complained.

"Look for something unusual."

"We had this discussion before," Junior responded.

"Yeah, yeah. Just keep looking. Keep looking."

"Holy shit!" they both yelled as they heard the chilling words, "Come here, you fat bastard."

"It's the bulls!" shouted Pat.

"It's Moose Miller," Junior whimpered.

"Come here, you son of a bitch," came the voice out of the darkness.

As they both turned slowly with their hands in the air to see who was talking to them, they froze . . . There was no one there.

"It's a spook!" Junior yelled as he turned and bolted for the door with Pat lumbering clumsily behind him. They burst out onto King Street, moving faster than either thought they could, running toward their car. Jumping behind the wheel, Junior started the engine as Pat fell into the front seat, barely shutting the door as they peeled out screeching on the cobblestones.

Lights came on in two houses as their curious occupants opened the windows and looked out to see a quiet, empty street, devoid of moving cars. Pat and Junior had escaped being seen as they raced up Van Brunt toward President Street and home. Junior proudly displayed the spring he still held in his hand. "No matter what . . . we got this. We got it."

"If it is what we think it is, get ready to be rich. Get ready to have the broads falling all over you. Get ready for Vegas." Pat was happy but still a little shook up over what had just occurred. "Now we gotta find the thing that makes the spring work."

"I ain't going back there, boss. No more. No way."

"You will if I tell you to. You unnerstand that?" Pat said sternly.

"I mean it . . . I ain't going back there." He was resolute.

"You're lucky, because I don't think we need to go back there to find it. What we gotta do is follow the Bird around for a few days and see what he has in his hands, especially when he goes over to see the Mick." Pat was pleased with himself for devising this plan of action.

"Yeah. That's good, boss. I like that." He breathed a sigh of relief. "But what are we looking for in Billy's hands?"

Pat spat out with extreme exasperation, "His Johnson. What do you think we'd be looking for?"

Junior shrugged at the question.

Pat shook his head in frustration as he said with exaggerated slowness, "We don't know what we are looking for, Junior. That's why we're gonna follow him around."

Junior thought for a moment and then responded with a simple "Okay."

ELEVEN

Dances with Bees

Billy Guarino left his apartment house at nine o'clock the next morning without noticing Junior standing partially hidden in a store doorway right across the street from his apartment building. The mobster began walking a little behind Billy, who he noticed was empty-handed, as he moved along just across the street. Billy went into John and Mary's candy store. Junior had to consider whether or not he should follow him in or not. Before he made his decision, he saw Pat walking from his observation point with a slice of watermelon in his hand, signaling him in an unusually animated way, indicating he should stay out of the store. At that moment, for some reason, a small swarm of bees landed on Pat's shoulders and went below the collar line. He swatted them, and they in turn started stinging the living hell out of him.

John was peering out the door of the store and started to laugh.

"What's up, John?" Billy wondered why he had suddenly burst into laughter.

"I'm looking at that silly bastard Pat Galucci doing some kinda stupid dance out on the sidewalk. He's waving his arms and pointing at something. Now he's stomping his feet and hitting himself on the back of the neck. Look at him." John was roaring with laughter. "Maybe he had a little bit of anisette in his coffee this morning."

Lulu and her husband Lou happened along, and she immediately joined in the action by clapping her hands in what she perceived to be the rhythm he was "dancing" to. "Hey, keep it up, Pat. You're doing great. I didn't know you could move like that." She complimented loudly as her husband just stood by her side with a disapproving look on his face. Both seemed to be ignored by the bees. They didn't even notice them.

"This guy is nuts, Lulu. Why're you encouraging him? He's acting like a dumb shit. Dancing in the street like this to no music. Stupid."

Doctor No was at it again with his negative and uninvited comments. Lulu paid no attention.

A small crowd started to gather around, and cars that were driving by slowed to a crawl. Some of the drivers began to shout laughing encouragement to the "dancing" mobster.

"What the hell is wrong with him, John?" Billy turned on his stool, looking out at Pat, wondering about the strange scene he was observing. "For a fat guy, he can really step."

Her hands on her hips, Mary chuckled and shook her head as she watched from the doorway. "Fool," was all she said, almost to herself.

Junior ran over to Pat and tried to help him after he realized that he was being stung repeatedly. Then they both sprinted to the candy store and practically knocked Mary down as they charged through the doorway. "Holy shit! Holy shit!" Pat shouted as he killed the last bee on his neck. "Gimme some ice or something," he pleaded as he sat on the stool, breathing heavily.

"What was it that you were doing out there, Pat?" John couldn't help but be nice at that moment, trying to suppress a laugh. "Here's some ice cubes in this towel."

Pat nodded his appreciation for the ice.

"It was bees, John," Junior responded, allowing Pat to catch his breath.

"I never saw bees do that around here before," Billy offered.

"They was probably attracted to Jimmy the Fruit Stand's watermelon," Pat gasped. "There must a' been a hundred thousand a' them little bastards." He ran the ice cubes across the back of his neck, trying to freeze the pain.

"I counted only about ten," commented Jimmy the Fruit Stand as he walked slowly into the store shaking his balding head, his perennial cap sitting comfortably upon it.

"Maybe you oughtta put that watermelon case in the basement with your shoes, Jimmy, instead of leaving it right in the front of the store," Mary opined with a slight chuckle, surmising what Jimmy was thinking.

"The store is too little to put it somewheres else, Mary. Wouldn't make a difference. Bees don't respect boundaries anymore. Ain't like it used to be." In his heart, Jimmy was happy with what the bees had done to Pat Galucci, but he knew he shouldn't laugh about it. In a way, it was payback for the way Pat had treated him.

"You know what, Pat? I've been thinking about an invention that —" Billy started to say.

"Yeah, I know all about your invention, Bird. And so does my father," Pat interrupted as he continued icing himself down the back of his shirt. "I know where you're going with this, Billy. You got some stupid piece a' shit thing that you and that crazy leprechaun on King Street think will automatically open convertible couches. And . . . what's that got to do with what just happened to me, anyways?" This was Pat's clumsy attempt at disguising his intense interest in what Billy and Harold had come up with.

"Nothing," Billy responded flatly after sipping his coffee.

"Then what are we talking about here?" Pat grumbled.

"We're talking about a new idea we have with flying insect execution."

"What?"

"Yeah . . . it started with my thinking that mosquitos are a major pain in the ass all summer long here. And flies are even worse for an even longer time than the mosquitos. Now seeing what happened to you today makes me add bees to the list." Billy looked straight ahead into the mirror that hung on the wall behind the counter. He could see Pat's wheels turning as he began to be played like a fiddle.

"What are you working on—a new giant blowtorch?" Pat laughed despite his pain. But inside his head were dancing thoughts of the additional money he could come into with this guy's weird head and ability to invent stuff. All he needed was to wait until it was real and then grab it. This was going to be as easy as pie. His mind was racing.

"Nah. No need to burn up the neighborhood, Pat. There's a much better way to do it than that."

"And that way is . . . ?"

"I'll let you know when we have the, uh, whatchamacallit? Uh, oh yeah . . . the unveiling," Billy said coyly.

"Maybe you need some financial backing on this, Billy boy," Pat offered with a warm, friendly tone, backed up with his toothy smile as he patted the Bird on the back.

"Don't need a dime. We got it all handled. Right, John?" Billy winked, turning his head toward the candy man, hoping he would pick up on his jest.

"Right, Billy!" John shot back with a big grin and a wink. "It's in the bank."

Pat got sucked into believing that John, and maybe Mary, were in partnership with the Bird on whatever he was coming up with. He immediately started plotting a way into this. He started scanning the store, looking for indications of what Billy was claiming.

"Can I use the bathroom?" Pat asked.

"Sure. Just go through that door over there and you'll see it."

Pat went into the small studio apartment attached to the rear of the store and scanned the entire area quickly, especially the door that led to the yard out back and the security-barred window that looked out onto it. He made a mental note of the layout. He entered the bathroom, scanning as much of the area as he could after washing his face and neck where the bee stings were swelling. "Sons of bitching bees," he grumbled to himself. The young mobster took his time before returning to the store proper. Again looking for anything that could be an indication of the new gadget that was in the pipeline.

As he walked back to the counter, he heard Billy saying, "I think the best way to describe this thing would be . . . like, this big vacuum cleaner thing and also a big wind fan. It would get rid of all the mosquitos and flies in South Brooklyn. We can't kill all the bees though."

"And why not?" Pat asked indignantly as he perched himself back on a stool.

"Because without bees, we ain't got no flowers or fruit." Billy's tone was professorial without him realizing it.

"And no Jimmy the Fruit Stand, neither," Pat said with a barb in his voice as he turned and looked at Jimmy. He paused, eyeing Jimmy, looking for a response that didn't come. "I'm sure that my father would love to know more about this bug killer, Billy," Pat said as he turned his attention back on Billy.

"Hey, Pat . . . wait a minute," John interjected. "I got a piece of this action too, ya know. Why ain't I getting an invite to visit with your father?"

"Oh, you're always welcomed to see the don. You know that without me having ta tell ya. Right, John?" Pat was caught off guard by John's question. He knew that his father liked John and Mary, and he didn't want word getting back to him that he had offended either of them. Billy knew this too and proceeded to start putting together a plan that would serve his adversary right for being such a greedy jerk.

"I'll keep your offer in mind, Pat, and will let you know where we're at with this one." He watched Pat's face for a reaction, and he got it when Pat's big nose flared, indicating he was getting excited.

"Where do you guys work on these inventions, Billy?" Jimmy the Fruit Stand asked quietly.

"Right now we use Harold's embalming room. It's always cool down there, and with the walk-in cooler we have room to test our stuff."

"Ain't no mosquitos in a cooler, Billy boy. Is there?" Pat asked like he had just discovered a big piece of science.

"Yeah, I guess you're right about that. We're thinking a movin' our lab to a space that Harold owns right next to the Greenwood Cemetery."

"That sounds creepy, Billy. Who would want to work there?" The young mobster was a bit anxious in his curiosity.

"And who would want to spy on us if we was there, too, eh?" Billy asked coyly.

"Yeah, I was wondering about that. And it's probably haunted like a funeral parlor could be." Pat was almost thinking out loud, and Billy picked up on it instantly.

"How do you know that?" Billy jumped on Pat's words.

"How do I know what?"

"About the hauntings in Harold's place."

"You kidding? Everybody knows that place is haunted. You can't be there after it closes for the night. That's when the spooks start moving around," Pat said mockingly.

"You ever been there after closing time?" Billy asked quickly.

"Sure," Junior blurted without thinking. Then tried to recover with "I mean somebody who has been there told me . . . uh, that."

"Really?" Billy faked a puzzled expression on his face. "I would love to talk with him or her about that, because I've had some scary shit happen there too. Real scary," he whispered for effect.

"Oh yeah, really?" Pat asked, trying to seem disinterested but not getting one over on anyone in the store with the exception of Junior. "You're trying to tell me that you believe in ghosts?"

"I'm not saying that, but I sure ain't saying that they don't exist." Billy was watching Pat's face intently in the mirror as he slowly sipped his coffee.

"I sure as all shit believe in them," John stated emphatically. "Especially after what happened here."

"What happened here, John?" Pat asked, his curiosity raised.

"I heard my dead mother-in-law call me one morning as I was opening up the store. It was still dark out. I think she's still hanging around here," John said, almost wishing that he hadn't mentioned it.

"Careful, John. Or else you're gonna have this one"—Pat nodded his head toward Junior—"pissing in his pants. That is, if he ever comes here after dark."

Junior started to respond to that, seeming annoyed, but then thought better and just dropped it.

Jimmy started nodding his head. "I gotta tell you something. But you gotta promise that you won't call me nuts." He looked around at everyone there, waiting for their agreement, and when it came, he said, "I was walking over to the bus stop one night after I had stayed here later than usual, and when I passed here, I heard something."

"What'd you hear?" Mary pressed him.

"I don't know for sure, but it was an old woman saying something about a beer."

"A beer?" John blurted out. "There you are, Mary. I told you I heard her. A beer." He shook his head excitedly.

"Yeah, a beer." Jimmy looked straight at Mary. "And I gotta tell you it sounded like your mother."

"That was her, Mary." John looked down and couldn't help but laugh, feeling vindicated. "She was always looking for a beer. Was she not?"

"Go away, the both of you. My mother wouldn't hang out here. If she was drinking a beer, it wouldn't be in here." She chuckled.

"Why do you say that, hon? She put many away right here in this very place," John said assuredly.

"That was because she couldn't travel far in her wheelchair. But now she's got no limitations. She can have a cold one anywhere she wants," Mary said lightly.

"Anyways, we got to get going." Pat, still in some pain, rose slowly from the stool and headed for the door with Junior following closely behind. "See yas all." He waved goodbye without turning back around. Junior just half smiled but said nothing as he shuffled slowly out the door.

After Pat and Junior were out of earshot, Billy cautioned, "John, you'd better make sure that you got this place wrapped up tight when you leave here every night. I think we woke up two sleeping tigers."

"Tigers may be a stretch. I would say maybe two sleeping monkeys. Better." John was delighted with his quip.

TWELVE

Brooklyn Monkey Business

"You see that shit, Junior?" Pat said as they walked toward his car that was parked just off Van Brunt Street far enough for no one in the candy store to notice.

"What shit?"

"You see, if you used your mind and listened when people was talking, you might pick up things."

"What things, boss? You're losing me here."

"Things like the new invention that the Bird and the Friendly Undertaker are coming up with." He nudged his cohort as he went on. "Can you imagine what this world would be like if there was no more flying bugs to bother people?"

"Yeah, I know that I would like that extremely much."

"So would millions a' others."

"Who can do that?" Junior asked innocently.

"Asshole! Weren't you just standing right there when me and the Bird was talking about his new invention?"

"Yeah, I was, but I wasn't really listening to what you guys was talking about."

"He was saying that him and the undertaker are working on an invention that will take out all the flying bugs in Red Hook."

"Those guys could be geniuses, ya know, boss? But yet they both seem like friggin' jerks to me."

"Jerks or geniuses, it don't matter. What matters is that what they got can make us rich if we can kinda make it like it's ours before they can get it on the market."

"How do we do that, boss?"

"Like we're doing with the automatic folding couch opener. We sneak into where they are coming up with this stuff, and when we see something close to being done . . . we grab it. Capeesh?"

"Yeah, I guess I do get it. You are always ahead a' the wave, boss. Makes life a real adventure." Junior was going back to being a sycophant, and it was working on Pat.

"Ya know, Junior, if you stick with me, I'm gonna make you rich . . . in a big way," he promised. "There's no reason why I wouldn't throw ya what you had coming if this all comes together." He laughed as he spoke words of comfort, which were unusual.

"So what's next on this?" Junior was now in a curious mode.

"We keep an eye on these guys. That's what's next, Junior. And you keep your mouth shut about this. We don't say nothin' to nobody. You got that?" He quickly reverted back to his real demeanor.

"What about ya father?"

"The old man don't need to know nothin' until we got somethin' to show him." Pat was emphatic.

Meanwhile, back at the store, Billy, John, and Mary were joking about the way Pat swallowed the "flying bug killer invention" hook, line, and sinker.

Mary asked, "What were you talking about that got Pat so into what you were saying, Billy? He looked like he was gonna climb onto your lap at one point during your conversation."

"I was telling him about this new machine that Harold and I are working on that will kill all the flying bugs all over the Hook and even beyond."

"Yeah, I heard that, but which part of it got him so wound up?" she asked, semi-controlling her laughter.

"It was when I explained to him that we was having to expand our operation to a place Harold owns, which is right next door to Greenwood Cemetery. Then I threw in that you and John were investing in this."

John asked slowly, very amused, "Is any of it true?"

"Nah. It's all bullshit. I love yanking his chain. He's the biggest *cafone* around, and he always thinks that he's the wisest guy in the room."

"That's why they call those people 'wise guys,' you know." John nudged Billy as he spoke. "And now we gotta be careful about how far we take this," he cautioned.

"What's making you say that, John?" Billy asked, now a bit concerned.

"You know those sneaky bastards better than me, Billy. You don't think they'll be nosing around here now, looking for this machine we supposedly got going?"

"You know, John, I got so caught up in the story that I didn't think about that. I'm sorry if this causes you a problem." Billy felt bad about drawing the store owners into his little prank.

"Do you think that Pat would be stupid enough to start hanging around here, trying to find out more about the machine?" Mary began to realize where this could be going. Then she dismissed it as being too ridiculous even for Fat Pat Galucci to actually run with it. "You know guys, I think we're giving Pat and his shadow a little more credit than they deserve. We don't need to be adding them to our daily list of worries. We got enough of those already. Let's just enjoy the idea that Billy really did get Pat going on this and made him act like the fool that he is."

Billy was glad that the conversation turned in a better direction.

Harold and Sylvio were beginning to form a relationship as the chatty bird began to look forward to the undertaker's generosity with the sunflower seeds he was giving him. He did so on an hourly basis as he coached Sylvio to repeat, "Come here." Harold spoke in a ghostly whisper, and it didn't take long for it to register in Sylvio's memory bank. His mimic was almost a perfect recording of Harold's eerie sounding words.

"That's it," he thought. Harold wanted Sylvio to say only the phrases he repeated over and over. However, Sylvio had a few phrases that were apparently emblazoned in his memory bank. Specifically, "Come here, you son of a bitch." This made Harold laugh whenever it passed through his ears.

What Harold had in mind was to volunteer to be Sylvio's "babysitter," which would bring him into his funeral parlor, then use him as a way to scare some people who he thought really needed some scaring. Like Pat and Junior. Harold should have been a comedian rather than an undertaker because he loved making people laugh as a result of his practical jokes.

Billy phoned his business partner, interrupting him in the middle of his training session with Sylvio. "Harold, I gotta tell ya something that's gonna make ya pee in your pants." He went on to tell him about the prank he had just hatched on Pat Galucci, and Harold loved it. "How do you think we can keep this going?" he asked, hoping Harold would come up with something surefire.

"We gotta start some neighborhood buzz, Billy. Neighborhood buzz is what we need here," he reiterated as the wheels in his head turned. "Who's the biggest rumormongers we know?"

"That's easy. It's gotta be Willie and his buddy Richard."

"And where can we find Willie and Richard?"

"At the Blue Bar."

"Then that's where we start." Harold was really liking this.

"So do you want to meet me there?"

"In a half hour or so?"

"Yeah, and let's you and me sit right next to Willie and talk about our 'new' invention, letting him eavesdrop what we are saying." Billy was liking the way this was coming together.

Willie and Richard were two black men who were childhood friends that grew up in the same proximity as Harold and Billy and were "real characters," according to anyone who knew them. Richard was fairly quiet and almost always agreed with everything Willie said, usually expressing his agreement with a nod of his head. Willie was more vocal but used a limited vocabulary. Like responding to most statements with "Sure, what then?" Which came out of his mouth as "Sho, wha' den?" And if he was asked if he knew certain people, his standard reply was, "Sho', I went to the same kinda, kinda college as him (or her)." Willie and Richard were loved by the people in the neighborhood, but they were also the biggest rumormongers alive at that time in Red Hook, often exaggerating the rumors they shared with the good people of the neighborhood. A fertile tool for Harold at that particular moment as he was preparing one of the greatest pranks of his life. Playing jokes on the unsuspecting was his greatest joy.

Willie and Richard both made a living as taxi drivers and usually worked evenings. They knew the city backwards and forwards because that was what was required of a successful "cabbie in those days.

Harold slid up on a stool next to the one Billy had climbed onto, next to Willie. He ordered and paid for two beers. He greeted Willie after surprising him with his rapid perching on the barstool with "Hey, man. How's things?"

Willie smiled as he eyed Billy and Harold, slowly answering, "Not much happening. Been here for a while today, that's why I'm saying they ain't too much happening."

"Yeah us too, but that may be changing soon." Billy told Willie, then turned his head and winked at Harold. "But ya know what?" He turned back toward Willie.

"No. I don't know much, Billy. But maybe Richard do."

Richard just shook his head in the negative, laughing. "No, Willie, I be thinking the same thing, ain't nothin' happenin' here. No, sir." He threw both his hands, clenched lightly in front of him, like a man reigning in two horses that were pulling a wagon. His laugh continued for a few seconds, warming the moment.

"What'chu doing, man? Do you think that it's easy doing nothin'?" Willie chided his buddy, nudging him gently with his elbow.

Harold stretched a bit as he leaned into the bar, looking past Billy while asking Willie and Richard, "What do you hear about Pat Galucci these days?"

"Only thing that he be an asshole. That's what I hear," Willie answered quickly.

"Why do you think you are hearing that?" Billy asked.

Willie shrugged his shoulders and said simply, "Because he an asshole. That's all."

"Yeah, that says a lot," Harold agreed. "You know that he's breaking our balls, right?" He paused before saying, "I have to do something about it."

"Sho. Wha' den?" Willie became more focused, sitting straight up on the barstool.

"I don't know yet, but we—Billy here and me—have to make sure he's not tapping into what we got going."

"Sho. Wha' den?"

"What then?" Harold shrugged his shoulders. "Maybe we start doing our inventing work at my other place next door to Greenwood Cemetery." He waited for Willie's response.

"That's some scary shit, Harold. Gimme the shakes just thinking 'bout it." Richard nodded his agreement. Willie was a thin man and Richard was a bit corpulent. Both had the same body language in reaction to Harold's statement . . . feigned shaking.

"Tell him what we hear about what people see at Greenwood at night, Willie. Go 'head, tell him," Richard chided.

"Tell me what, Willie?" Harold asked.

"He be talking 'bout what people saying about what goes on there at night." He shuddered as he spoke. "Richard, you don't be needing to bring up that shit."

"What we talking about here, Willie? These gentlemen need to be knowing what's going on there at night before they get the shit scared from them by what they see," Richard advised.

"Okay then, this be what Richard referring to," Willie said resignedly. "I don't like talking 'bout stuff like this because it might bring these folks to my doorstep. Unnerstand?"

Billy responded immediately with "Yeah, really?" He was caught up in the moment and what Willie was saying.

"They say that there are folks wandering around that cemetery late at night that shouldn't be there. No how." Willie shook his head and looked down, not liking what he was saying. "These folks are the spirits of their bodies lying beneath where they are wandering. Give me the creeps."

"Not good news if you believe in ghosts, Willie," Harold commented. "But I don't believe in ghosts." He paused a moment. "But you know, I have heard things at night when I worked late at the parlor." He watched his words register with Willie.

"Then why you gonna be working so close to the cemetery, Harold?"

He answered without missing a beat. "I don't know. Maybe it's just a matter of needing more room for the development of the next invention."

"You next invention? What's that?" Willie's curiosity was breaking through.

Then Harold nailed it without answering the question. "Can't talk about it yet, Willie, but I think that we will be moving our experiments to my Greenwood Cemetery place."

"Sounds crazy, Harold, but never ain't much sane 'bout you anyways." He chuckled disarmingly.

Harold winked at Willie. Then a big smile spread across his leprechaun-like face as he nudged Billy, indicating that they should be leaving. "See ya guys," Harold said as they exited the bar.

"You take care," Willie responded, then turned to Richard. "We can check on his place at night whenever we get a fare nearby. If yo' want to do that."

"You speak fo' yourself, Willie. Ain't no way I be doin' that. I ain't crazy."

"You don't want to help those fellas?" Willie was upset by what he was hearing. "They sho' would help us."

"Hell no, man. I be scared outta my mind to go near that cemterry durin' the nighttime." Richard shook his head back and forth quickly to emphasize his words.

"You'll be changing yo' mind, Richard. Yo' wait an' see."

"You be waitin' a long time fo' that to happen. Long time," Richard reiterated.

Harold drove with Billy to his Greenwood Cemetery location. They were listening to the Beatles's "We Can Work It Out" on the radio. "You know, Harold, if everyone would take this song to heart, we would have a better world," Billy said almost without thought as he listened.

"Almost everybody. Let's don't go overboard here, Billy. Ya gotta keep in mind that Pat Galucci is still part of 'everybody,' so let's don't get too far ahead of ourselves." He chuckled mischievously as he nudged Billy with his boney elbow, not taking his eyes off the road.

They pulled up in front of a dreary-looking cinderblock building, and after parking, they walked slowly to the door and inside. It smelled of chemicals because this was where Harold did some of his embalming, and that made Billy feel a little queasy.

He looked around at the metal tables and the hoses attached to several machines, and it gave him the creeps. "You sure that we should be using this place to build our anti-bug device, Harold?"

Harold shrugged his shoulders. "And why not? We have plenty of room here. You thinking this won't work for some reason?"

"I don't know. It makes me feel a little funny. You know, respect for the dead and all that stuff."

"I promise you that I won't work on any bodies here while we're in the process of putting the whole thing together. Will that make you feel better?"

"Yeah. I suppose it will, Harold."

"Let's figure out if this can work first. We're gonna have to do a lot of experimenting with fans and electric hot plates to start."

"Where we gonna get the flying bugs to try it out with?"

"Let's get it built and then we'll take it down to Red Hook and set it up in an empty lot that's full of dog shit. The rest will take care of itself." Harold smiled proudly. "Just think of what this could do for humanity, Billy."

"And . . . what it could do for our wallets. This is something we pulled out of the air, and now it's really becoming something," Billy crowed.

"But keep in mind here the thing we really have going for us is the automatic folding couch opener. That's what we gotta keep close to our chests and out of the hands of Fat Pat."

"Ya know, Harold, ya got me thinking here that maybe we should put our experiments right here. Like maybe getting the spring installed on the couch and having it here too."

"Why the sudden change of heart about this place, Billy? You've been saying that it gives you the creeps and all." Harold was truly puzzled.

"Yeah, sure it gives me the deep creeps. If it gives me that—now, think about this without bein' insulted an' stuff—most normal people should feel the same way as me."

"Where're you going with this, Billy?"

"That's simple. It will keep nosey assholes outta here." Billy smiled broadly.

"Like who're you talking about?" He placed his hands in his pockets and leaned forward in Billy's direction, laughing.

"I gotta tell you that?"

Harold shook his head as he continued laughing with the thought rolling through his head of how much fun he could have with this. "Makes sense. Yeah, I like it."

"You getting my full meaning?"

"Maybe yes. Maybe no. Give me a rundown."

"You know the rumors about this cemetery and what goes on here at night. Right?" Billy pointed at the window that faced the cemetery proper.

"I've heard stories . . . sure." Harold was liking this more and more, and he started working on a plan to expand his babysitting duties with Sylvio and what could come of that with the "nosey assholes" Billy referred to. Yeah, this could be a goldmine of practical jokes, which would make Harold the happiest man in Red Hook.

THIRTEEN

The Midnight Riders

Word was rolling through John and Mary's store clientele that something big was on the horizon for the Friendly Undertaker and Billy the Bird. It was spreading rapidly and was soon picked up by Junior, who immediately reported it to Fat Pat.

"You picked up on this . . . how?" was the underboss's reaction.

"It's on the street."

"What 'street,' Junior?"

"You know . . . the candy store . . . uh, that street."

"John and Mary's?"

"Yeah."

Pat thought for a moment before saying, "That's what I picked up that time when John was talking with Billy about something big that they was into as . . . 'partners.' " He emphasized "partners" with an outward breath.

"What do you think we should do?"

"That's easy, Junior. We find out what they got going and then we grab it from them as soon as they got it done." He laughed as he looked in a full-length mirror, checking out the new suit he had just tried on after having it altered. He kept his gaze on the mirror as he asked, "What d' ya think?"

"About what?"

"About the moon having pigeons." He released another exasperated breath. "What's a matter with you? We have these two jerks inventin' stuff and just begging for someone to take it from them. No problem here, Junior . . . all ya gotta do is use your head, and you'll be like me," Pat said, smiling smugly while tapping his forehead with one extended finger.

Junior thought, "And that's something I should want?" But he didn't dare verbalize it.

"So what d' ya think? Should I have these pants pegged?" Pat asked while he continued viewing himself in the mirror.

"Ah . . . I don't know about that. Pegged pants ain't that much in style no more."

"Not in style? What ya talkin' about? Pegged pants have always been in style, ever since I can remember," Pat replied, annoyed by Junior's comment.

"Not since the hippies started with their bell-bottoms bullshit," Junior said, looking away from Pat because he didn't want to have to look him in the eye.

"Screw those dirt bags; I wear what I wear when I want to wear it. So I'm going with pegging these pants." He stepped off the tailor's platform after the pants on his new sharkskin suit had been chalked by a smiling Sy "the Tailor" for additional tailoring of the hems.

Pat changed back into his slacks and with a head signal, left the tailor's shop with Junior following behind. He slowed enough for his underling to catch up with him before saying, "We gotta start watching things at John and Mary's more close by keeping our ears to the ground so that we can make our moves at the right time."

"Yeah, keep our ears on the ground." Junior chuckled as he spoke.

"What ya laughing at, asshole?" Pat spat out, which threw Junior off a bit because he was only trying to be funny.

"I'm not laughing at you, boss," Junior responded apologetically. "I was jus—"

"Just showing what a jerk you are at times, Junior."

Junior thought about a comeback but elected to remain quiet and let Pat's anger pass. They got into the Cadillac and headed for John and Mary's.

When they arrived, Lou and Lulu were discussing an upcoming event at the VFW Post and the parade that Lulu was going to march in with the VFW Women's Auxiliary. She said, "The Visitation band will be leading the way, and there were a few neighborhood store owners who will drive their cars in it. Harold is even going to drive his hearse in it for the first time ever. That's really big, ya know, because it's the only time ever that he's done that."

"I don't like it," Lou muttered, his eyes looking down, motioning with his hands to accentuate his statement. "It looks stupid. You know how friggin' crazy that Mick is. What makes you think he won't pull something dumb and screw up the whole parade?"

"He won't do something like that. He's a nice man. You can tell by the way he likes playing jokes on people. He's not gonna do anything to mess up everybody. Come on, Lou."

"Hey, don't say I didn't warn ya. That's all I got to say. That's it. Period." He made a motion with his hands like an umpire calling a play safe.

"What the hell is Harold doing with a funeral hearse in a parade?" John joined in the conversation. Nobody answered, so he continued, "I believe that he'll pull some shit and get everybody going." He chuckled as he poured water into the coffee machine.

Now, it should be kept in mind that the VFW Post parades were a big deal in Red Hook, Brooklyn. Even Carl the cop stood at attention when it passed by. Lulu would have none of this pessimism. Nothing was going to rain on her parade. Not even her husband, the original Doctor No.

What nobody knew at that point was that Harold had indeed planned something for that parade that would send the whole neighborhood into a frenzy. And the plan had Harold staying at his Greenwood Cemetery location late at night, not only working on the bug-killing machine with Billy the Bird but also working on completely revamping one of his funeral hearses into a vehicle that could be driven with him lying flat, almost at floor level, so it would look like no one was driving it. He kept this little ploy totally to himself so that it would be a total surprise to everyone in the Hook and would leave a lasting impression on all. Oh yeah, a very lasting impression.

"What d' ya know? What d' ya hear?" Pat asked Junior when he got back in the car after going into John and Mary's for a pack of smokes.

"Nothin' really, boss. Lou and Lulu were talkin' about the next VFW Post parade that's scheduled soon. Actually, they was kinda arguing over some stupid shit."

"What kinda stupid shit?"

"Well, Lulu is telling everybody in the store the Friendly Undertaker is gonna drive a funeral hearse in the parade."

"A funeral hearse? Ya gotta be kiddin' me. Why the hell would anyone want to be doing that?"

Junior shrugged his shoulders. "I don't know. But if anyone in the world was gonna do that and you asked me who, I gotta tell ya it would be the Mick."

Pat absorbed Junior's words as he ran a series of thoughts through his mind. Thoughts like what the reasoning would be behind the person in charge of the parade allowing a loony tune like that even watch the parade, much less be in it. "Are you sure you heard right, Junior? A funeral hearse?"

"Oh yeah, boss. That's what I heard."

"This is too nuts to even talk about. But ya know that little Mick bastard is always up to something, and it's usually got a message attached to it."

"Like what kinda message?"

"Oh, I don't know. Maybe somethin' like it's a way to roll out the bug-killing machine when everybody's watching. I'll bet that's what this is all about. Yeah, he's gonna make a big splash in that parade." Fat Pat was on a roll as he started constructing a story in his head about how Harold was going about this. "He's probably close to being done with his bug-killing machine, or maybe he's gonna have his automatic couch in that hearse ready for all the world to see."

"So what do we do with this, boss?"

Pat touched his temple with his index finger. "We use our noggins, Junior."

"But what do we do?"

"We spy like a son of a bitch. We follow his ass everywhere and make sure he don't get wise that we are doing this. It won't be long until he tips his hand. Let's take a ride past the King Street funeral parlor and see if he's there."

———

Harold wasn't at the parlor. Nor was Billy. Nor was Sylvio. Billy was home reading an encyclopedia on the world of bugs. Harold was at the Greenwood Cemetery location with Sylvio in his cage listening to Harold say over and over again, "Come here. Come here, you son of a bitch." Harold used his relaxation time with his newly found little buddy to create the potential for mayhem in the paper gangster world of Fat Pat Galucci. Visions of bad guys being scared out of their minds were dancing in his head as he continued repeating to Sylvio, "Come here. Come here, you son of a bitch."

It was dark, very dark, when Pat rolled his Cadillac to a halt about a half-block from Harold's Greenwood Cemetery building. "Let's take a look-see if that crazy little bastard is here." They moved gingerly down the street, and as they approached they saw a limousine parked right in front of the building that Pat was certain belonged to Harold. He nudged Junior and whispered, "That's it. One a' his cars. Right there." He pointed knowingly.

"Whatta we do now?" the underboss's underboss asked as they both looked up and down the empty street.

"We go aroun' the back a' the building and see what we can see." There was an unlocked gate not twenty feet from where they stood that they used to get closer so they could peer into the building where Harold was bending a spring and looking at it with great intensity.

"Why do you think this gate isn't locked, boss?" Junior asked suspiciously.

"Why lock anything around here? Who breaks into a cemetery at night? Right?" he said smugly.

"Us. That's who," Junior answered immediately, without thought.

"That's right, Junior. Us, who are on our way to fame and fortune." He was more and more certain that he was on the right trail with this. "We just watch this guy, and when he's almost done with whatever he's got ready to roll out, we grab it. We grab it, and my old man will bankroll us with a lawyer who will get it through the patent office. And bingo, Junior, we are on our way to the good life. Alls we gotta do is keep our eyes and ears open, and that stupid jerk will do the rest for us without even knowing he did it—uh, until we roll it out."

Junior and Pat peered into Harold's building, standing on their tiptoes and straining their necks to get a peek in. It took a while for their eyes to adjust to the pitch blackness of the night. Suddenly, a light was thrown on the area near where Pat and Junior were watching. Pat signaled Junior to get down, not wanting to be seen. They retreated farther into the cemetery so as to avoid being discovered.

But they were discovered—by someone standing a short distance from them. With his dark taxi-driver clothes and dark skin, he was practically invisible to the prying eyes of the paper gangsters. Willie, hiding behind a tree big enough to keep him out of sight but still close enough to hear their conversation, smiled as he watched and listened. He had decided to learn what was really going on at that funeral parlor that had people in the Hook talking.

FOURTEEN

Willie

The next day, Billy met up with Harold at John and Mary's for coffee and some planning.

"What'll it be?" Mary asked, smiling brightly from behind the counter where she stood with her hands on her hips.

"I'll take a cup and one a' them onion rolls right there." Billy pointed at one of several sitting in the glass case next to the coffee pots.

"Just coffee for me, Mary," Harold said as he was focused on the obituaries in the *Daily News*. "Nothing today," he complained as he put the paper down on the stool next to him and shook his head.

"And that's supposed to be bad?" Billy asked.

"Sure. For me it is. I have to keep the lights on." He folded the paper.

"Hey, John, come here a minute," Harold said as he pulled his tape measure out his pocket and got off the stool, starting around the counter.

"Go on, you crazy son of a bitch, and put that tape measure where the sun don't shine." John chuckled as he smiled broadly, backing slowly away from Harold, not knowing how far he was going to go with this.

They were all laughing at John's comment as Carl "Shackles the

Cop" came through the door. "Mary, Mary, Mary." He greeted her and turned, saying with a nod, "John, John, John." He sat down one stool over from Harold as he continued, "Harold, Harold, Harold," and then "Billy, Billy, Billy."

All four chorused, "Carl, Carl, Carl."

He signaled John for a cup of coffee by mimicking someone sipping coffee. "What's new, folks?"

"Not much," came Harold's response. "Where are all the bodies, Carl?" he asked dryly.

"What bodies?" Carl was puzzled.

"I just checked the obits, and there is no one who kicked off within eight miles of this place. We need bodies Carl. We need bodies!" Harold mocked sadness and frustration, looking down while shaking his head from side to side.

"Harold, Harold, Harold. You gotta have patience, my friend. Everybody dies." He laughed quietly. "Remember that line from the old movie *Body and Soul*, where John Garfield's character says to the mob hitman after he doesn't throw the fight he was supposed to throw that the mob had bet on heavily? 'What are ya gonna do to me, Johnny? Kill me? Everybody dies.' That's what Garfield says to the Torpedo." Carl took off his cap and set it on the counter in front of him.

"Carl, Carl, Carl. That's in the movies, not real life," Harold responded, now smiling slyly. "Besides, what's so bad about dying when we all know what's waiting at the other end?"

"I think it's pretty good up there." Billy joined the conversation, pointing heavenward.

"So you don't mind dying then, Billy?" Carl asked between sips of coffee.

"I didn't say I minded dying. No, I wasn't talking about me," Billy retreated.

Harold sensed a chance to pull one of his signature pranks as he got off his stool and began measuring Billy with his tape. Billy jumped off his stool and started backing up, hands in front of him, shaking his head no as everyone in the store burst into laughter.

Jimmy the Fruit Stand came through the front door for his morning coffee, on the way to open his store. As was his habit, he began to say something starting in the middle of a sentence. "And I was sure he was wrong." He looked at everyone in the place, going from one to the other.

"What?" Carl asked.

"Of course!" responded Jimmy with a quiet laugh.

"Of course what?" Billy asked, looking confused.

Jimmy shrugged. "The thing." He paid Mary for his coffee, tipped his cap, and went on his way.

"What the hell was he talking about?" asked Harold as he started to follow Jimmy out the door with his tape measure ready in both hands. He came face-to-face with Fat Pat Galucci, who was coming through the door with Junior close behind.

Pat grunted, "Good morning," as he pointed toward the coffee pot as a signal he wanted coffee. Then he turned and pointed at Junior and put up two fingers, indicating he wanted another cup for his underling.

"What are you doing there, Pat? You learning sign language?" Harold asked with a puzzled expression after turning around and following the paper gangster back into the store.

"What are you talking, Harold? What sign language?"

"I saw you pointing at the coffee pot, then making a sign like you were drinking something. Then you point at this guy and make a peace sign. What? Are you a hippie now?"

"An' what are you? A wise-ass?" Pat became menacing.

"Hey. We don't want no trouble here," John warned, sensing Pat's anger. "Harold's only kidding with you."

Pat caught himself as he realized that Carl was watching him and looking like he was getting ready to stand up between them. "Oh, I'm only kidding, John. You know me. I love this little guy."

"That didn't look like love to me," Carl said, looking Pat up and down without an expression on his round face. "What's the matter? You get up on the wrong side of the bed today?"

"No, Officer. No, no. I was just trying to be funny in my own way. That's all." He turned his face toward Harold. "Right, Harold? You know that, right?" The menace was still quietly spilling through in his voice and eyes.

Harold smiled cynically. "No, I don't know that."

This threw Pat for a second, but he recovered with, "Hey, John, I'm buying Harold's coffee just to show there's no hard feelings. Okay?"

Harold didn't reply; he just raised his cup in response and sat back up on his stool.

Pat forced a smile. "Johnny, make those coffees for me and Junior to go. We wish we could stay for a while, but we have business."

Now with his coffee and Junior's coffee in hand, he said very politely, "Hey, Billy, can I have a word with you?" He nodded his head toward the outside, inviting Billy to go there. Billy looked at Harold and then Mary with concern in his eyes, but he followed Pat and Junior outside.

Pat told Billy that his father wanted to see him. "Today!"

"What's he want with me?"

"He'll tell you when you get there."

"What time?"

"One o'clock."

"At the club?"

"Yeah, at the club. Any place else you ever seen him?" Pat was annoyed by the question.

"Okay, Pat. Tell him I'll be there."

"Like you got a choice, asshole?" Pat snickered with a grin.

Billy shook his head no and walked back into the store, deep in thought, wondering what the don wanted him for.

"What's up, Billy?" Harold asked.

"Not sure."

Carl swiveled on his stool toward Billy. "You don't look happy. What's bothering you, kid?" The expression on Billy's face gave away the fact that he was realizing he had probably painted himself into a corner when he last met with Don Galucci only because he was trying to buy himself some time. And now the don was summoning him to a meeting that he had been hoping he wouldn't ever have to have. He realized that he might not only be getting himself in a jam but he could be doing that to Harold as well. His mind raced, trying to come up with something he could tell Don Galucci. Like maybe the experiment with the automatic sofa bed opener had failed, and they shut down the whole project.

But then that would mean they couldn't do anything more with it for fear of double-crossing an important mob figure. His and Harold's life wouldn't be worth a subway token then. He would have to level with Harold and see what his position on this would be. This was something he did not want to do, but there was no other option.

His mind shifted to the thought of possibly telling Don Galucci that Harold and he had formed a secret partnership with Carl and it had to be kept secret, really secret. Followed immediately by the thought that maybe he could offer the don a tribute—a one-time payment—and throw in naming the couch-opening device after his wife.

At that exact moment, Billy felt the walls suddenly closing in with Pat all of a sudden being just about everywhere he was. He knew he had to come up with something but what exactly that something was made it difficult. One thing he didn't know was that Willie the taxi driver was now in the mix, and that added a brand-new dynamic to the equation for all concerned.

At that exact moment, Willie the taxi driver came waltzing in just as Billy had taken his seat back on the stool at the counter.

"Hi, Willie," greeted Mary. "How've you been?"

"Been good, Mary. You?"

"I'm good too, thank you. You haven't been around much lately, and some people have been asking about you."

"Sho, wha' den?" Willie's most uttered phrase accompanied a quizzical expression.

"Not much else. They get to thinking that maybe you moved away or something." Mary smiled with her words.

"Me move away?" Willie chuckled warmly. "They ain't no other place for Willie. This my home, Mary."

"Willie, I got something I want to ask you." Harold got off his stool and walked toward Willie as he pulled his tape measure from his pocket.

"Cut out that shit, Harold. You know Old Willie be here lots mo' time than you be here." Willie laughed as he backed away from Harold and half stumbled backwards as Carl caught him.

Harold helped him to stand back up straight.

"I got somethin' you best be knowing, Harold," Willie said as he formed a huddle that included Carl and Harold. "That Pat Galucci an' his buddy be spying on you. They be looking in the window at your Greenwood Cemetery place."

Harold said, "You're shitting me. When did they do that?"

"Other night, Harold."

"Other night when, Willie?" Harold was upset.

"Other night when ol' Willie was poking around, trying to watch out fo' you 'cause I be hearing things."

No one had been paying attention to the fact that standing by the magazine rack in the back of the store was Jerry "Red," quietly scanning the magazines and just happening to hear Willie's words. He saw Billy put his finger to his lips, cautioning Willie to stop talking.

Willie looked at Jerry, catching Billy's action.

"Can we go back in the kitchen, John?" Harold asked as Jerry put the magazine he was scanning back on the rack and hurriedly left the store.

"Uh-oh, Willie. That wasn't good," Harold uttered, very concerned.

"You mean Jerry?" Willie looked puzzled.

"Yeah."

"Nah. He's a good guy. We went to the same kinda, kinda college together." Willie's second most used phrase.

"That son of a bitch didn't even finish high school. Much less go to college," John volunteered his opinion of Jerry.

"I'm not liking this," Billy said quietly as he wiped his forehead with his hand, realizing how much of the conversation he had heard.

By the time Billy was sitting before Don Galucci, he was totally unnerved, and he still did not have an excuse to offer regarding his and Harold's invention and why he hadn't been able to bring it to the senior Galucci by then. He found himself wishing that he had never gotten himself involved in this venture.

"Hey, kid. Whatchu doing these days?" The don entered the room where Billy sat woefully expecting things to start unraveling with the father of his archenemy Pat Galucci. "What's a matter with you?" He grunted as he took his usual seat in the big chair behind his desk. "You're looking pale, like you don't feel good. Don't you feel good, kid?"

"No, Don Galucci. I'm okay. Maybe a little tired."

"Tired? From what, Billy? You ain't been working. What is it that makes you tired?"

"No, nothing. I'm getting ready to go back to work on the docks as soon as the doctor clears me to do that." Billy had been living on workmen's compensation since he hurt himself unloading a ship. Don Galucci had helped him with getting his claim taken care of. Without his help, Billy would have been out of luck. This was just one more reason why he didn't want to get on the wrong side of him. He was wishing he could just walk away from the whole thing but also knew that he had to find a way to fix this. And fix it quickly.

"Ya know, kid, I've been thinking." The robust don looked at Billy and moved around in his big leather desk chair. He took his lighter from his trouser pocket and flicked it at the end of his cigar. "We may have something here that will make it no longer necessary for any of us to have to work anymore." He opened his arms and smiled broadly, looking at Billy through the squinted eyes of a happy man. "I got a feelin' about this."

"Yeah." Billy half stammered back, shaking his head with a certain degree of uncertainty.

"What's a matter, Billy? You don't look comfortable." The don put his feet up on the desk as he let out a sigh.

"No. No, Don Galucci, I'm very relaxed here."

"I ain't convinced of that, kid." The don waved his hand, dismissing Billy's response. "Not convinced at all."

"Can I say somethin'?" Pat Galucci requested from the chair he was occupying immediately behind Billy.

"No you can't. Not while I'm talking here." He threw his son a look that spoke volumes regarding his interruption. "Look, Billy, I think it's time we bring your invention partner into this and come to an agreement so that we can get this going. You know I'm not getting any younger."

Billy shook his head yes in response but kept his eyes down, avoiding the elder Galucci's eyes, which he felt were burning into him. He was surprised at the don's awareness of the progress he and Harold had made on the coach opener.

"So let's get your buddy in here and close this deal."

Billy's stomach sank at the sound of those words. He was filled with dread at the prospect of having to bring Harold into the conversation with Don Anthony Galucci, the man who ruled Red Hook. Who wouldn't appreciate pranks being played on him.

"When do you want this to happen?" Billy asked slowly.

"The twelfth of never," Pat interjected from his place behind Billy.

"What are you? An idiot?" The don spoke to his son.

"No, Pop. I'm just being funny. You know." He gestured with his hands in front of him, palms up.

"Yeah, I know. You come with that shit? And what are you, Johnnie what's-his-name all of a sudden? The twelfth of never?" His eyes flared for a moment as he directed, "You!" and pointed at his son. "You stop your shit and get yourself into an attitude with Billy here that makes you stop acting like he's a slug. He's gonna make us all rich. You get that? Tell me you understand."

"Oh yeah, Pop. I know what you're saying . . . totally." Pat grinned, trying to mask his anger over his father taking Billy's part and not his. "I don't get this," he thought. "Is the old man bringing this guy into the Family?"

"Billy, I want you to bring Harold in here so we can figure out who's going to be who in this arrangement." Don Anthony Galucci blew cigar smoke past his chubby lips that were forming a smile.

"When?" Billy asked, his eyes downcast.

"Call him now."

"I think he's at the morgue picking up a body right now."

"You think? Or you know?"

"I think."

"Call him," the don urged.

"Sure." Billy got up and walked over to the big desk that dominated the entire room. He dialed the number that he knew Harold would not be at. "No answer, Don Galucci." He laid the phone back into its cradle.

"Okay, let's do this: you bring him here tomorrow morning. Say ten o'clock. It won't take long, and we'll have a deal we can all live with." He stood up and walked over to Billy, who in turn stood up. He patted Billy on the back, shook his hand, and escorted him to the door. "See you tomorrow at ten, kid." He smiled as Billy walked out the door.

"That's good, Pop," Pat said as he tried to muster a smile.

"Where's Junior? I wanna speak with him."

"About what, Pop?" Pat asked uncomfortably.

"That's my business. Get him in here. Now!" He took a drag on his cigar. "You stay outside. Just Junior in here." He pointed at the door.

Within seconds, Junior came in and was directed to a chair directly across the desk from the don, who told him to keep an eye on his "asshole son" before he made the whole deal go away.

"But, Don Galucci, I kinda thought that Pat was my boss," he said awkwardly, totally confused by the don's directions. "It would feel stupid for me to try doing . . . Uh, uh, I don't know what to say . . . all due respect . . . I mean . . . you know."

"I don't give a shit about how stupid you feel; my son is more stupid. You keep an eye on him every minute a' the day over the next few days."

"What happens if he decides to not wanna do what I tell him?"

"He'll listen to you. Don't worry about that," the don assured him.

"Whatever you say, boss." Junior was almost beside himself from being placed in the middle of the big and current don and the future don. He was totally compromised at this point, and now he had to tell the boss about what Jerry heard at John and Mary's store.

When Junior finished the story, the don said, "So you're telling me that this black guy, Willie the Cabbie, has something on you two assholes?" He folded his arms and leaned toward Junior, anger growing in his eyes.

"Well, we was just spying on the Mick at his place near the cemetery and didn't see the black guy who was watching us all the time, watching the Mick too. It was all very innocent, boss. We was just standing there in the dark, doing nothing."

"Very innocent. Very innocent? Just standing there in the dark."

Don Galucci began pacing the room, repeating the words "very innocent" in a whisper until he turned and asked Junior, "What was Willie doing watching the Mick? Is he planning on doing something with this too? What else did Jerry tell you, Junior?"

Swallowing hard, Junior continued, "Don Galucci . . . I gotta tell you this . . . I'm sorry to have to do it . . . but he was talking with Carl the Cop in John and Mary's and telling Billy, Harold, and John and Mary about us looking in the window."

"So this guy is a rat, huh? You know what we do with rats, right, Junior?"

"Yeah, I get that, boss. But you saying you want me to take care of him?"

"Yeah I do, but not yet. Maybe we just scare him a little bit. Sort of convince him that talking with a cop ain't the smartest thing for a guy to do. Especially when that conversation takes place on our turf and it's about our deal. What's he trying to do—get a taste too, or is he just gonna grab it and run?"

Junior was now really conflicted because he liked Willie and didn't want to see him get hurt over this. "Yeah, I see what you're saying boss, but—"

"You see that, do you, Junior?" The don stomped his foot. "I don't want to hear no 'buts'!"

Junior said with his head down, "How do you want me to handle this, Don Galucci?"

"I want you to concentrate on keeping an eye on my idiot son. Keep him in line and also keep him from letting his temper make him do something stupid and screw up this whole thing." He looked intently at Junior as he drew on his cigar so hard that the light in the tip ash reflected in his eyes. "This thing is an opportunity we can't miss. Especially by him doing something stupid."

"I hear ya, boss, but how do I do that?" Junior had now transferred his loyalty from son to father, and he was beginning to feel more important than he had ever felt as an underling to the younger Galucci. And yet he felt a huge conflict brewing in his world. A world that was now filled with challenges and questions.

FIFTEEN

Who's the Boss Here?

"Hey, what are you doing?" Harold held a small cracker under Sylvio's beak as he repeated those words over and over. The bird, perched on the desk lamp in Harold's office in the King Street funeral parlor, looked at the cracker and then at Harold and then at the cracker and then at Harold. Over and over Harold repeated the phrase and Sylvio remained silent, but his interest in the cracker was growing by the minute. As was his agitation.

This went on for almost an hour, and Harold was getting tired and a bit disappointed that the parrot wouldn't parrot, so he decided to take a break and make himself a cup of hot tea. He opened the newspaper and started to read an article on tin and how using it in combination with steel brought it greater flexibility. He reread the article and then thought for a while about how this could bring him the ultimate spring. One that could be used on all sizes of convertible couches and maybe even convertible car tops. This process usually fed his genius and caused him to be so focused on whatever he was focusing on that he couldn't stop the experiments in his head until they were actually tested. He knew that they were close to being ready to test the spring, and the only unknown now was how much time should be spent on mixing the tin with the steel. He felt that he already had what was necessary as far as the mechanism for opening and closing the couches was concerned, and now all that was left was the electric motor adaptation that would activate the arm and spring. But this new ingredient of tin might be worth trying, even though it could delay the project a bit.

Billy the Bird was handling the remote, and it looked like he had done it by his using a receptor from a TV set that changed channels. The only drawback was that just jiggling coins in one's pocket could activate the device. Maybe that fact would mean mixing the tin with steel might not be a good idea in that a couch rapidly opening or closing could be dangerous for the mothers of Red Hook and, eventually, the state, the country, and the world.

"Hey, what are you doing?" Harold said again, hoping Sylvio would repeat his words.

But that did not happen. Sylvio flapped his wings wildly and paced back and forth. Something was not right with the spirited and contentious bird, and whatever it was did not register with the undertaker-scientist.

Pat Galucci snapped his fingers as he walked past Junior, signaling that he should follow him. And follow him he did as they walked out of the club house on President Street toward Pat's Cadillac that was parked at the curb. The sun was retreating in the sky, and Pat had decided that he was going to get to the center of things by pushing his way into the partnership between the Bird and the Friendly Undertaker. He felt it was time he did so, and he just knew that his father would finally give him the respect he deserved for getting this done.

"What are we doing, boss?" Junior asked, dreading what he knew was coming next.

"We're off to see the wizard." He laughed at his own joke as he pointed his finger toward the car. "Come on. We got business with Mr. O'Reilly, and that requires us to be in his presence."

Junior was searching for a way to tell Pat that his father had ordered him to keep him away from the Friendly Undertaker. That was not going to be easy. "Uh, boss, I think you had better talk with your father before we leave," he stuttered.

"Why? Where are you getting that from?" Pat was confused by Junior's words.

"Uh, just go talk with him. Uh, please."

"Okay. I'll be right back." He walked off to talk with his father again, a bit puzzled.

Within two minutes, he came roaring back with his face lobster red and fury in his voice. "So you are now the boss of me?" He leaned into Junior with disbelief flowing from his face. "The boss of me?"

"Uh, look. All I know is that your father, the don, told me to keep an eye on you and keep you from blowing this deal. What am I supposed to do, Pat? Tell him no? Come on." He shrugged his shoulders with a "what can I do about it?" gesture, looking very uncomfortable.

"Don't let it go to your head, asshole. You better not let that happen," Pat growled with fury.

"As far as I'm concerned, you are still my boss. All I'm doing now is what your father told me to do."

"You better say that. You better know who's your boss. Doesn't matter what my father says for you to do." He looked menacingly at Junior with fire in his eyes. "You got that? Right?"

"Yeah, right."

"I need to know that you mean it, Junior. I need to know that you ain't gonna try to cut my balls off." He stared at Junior with a growing intensity.

"Why would I do that, Pat? This is just a temporary arrangement, and as soon as we got the deal locked in, it all goes back to the way it used to be."

"It better." Pat looked away from his former underling.

"Hey, what are you doing?" Sylvio finally squawked, but it was very much like a sound you would have expected coming out of a parrot. This wasn't his usual perfect mimicking of the voices he heard.

Harold repeated the phrase back to Sylvio. Then Sylvio repeated the phrase, only this time he sounded exactly like Harold.

"Finally!"

"Finally!" Sylvio repeated in Harold's voice.

"Now it's time to finish the 'invisible driver' equipment for the big parade," he muttered to himself. Harold was seeing his greatest prank ever coming to fruition with his driverless ghost vehicle. He had installed a radio control device in the steering wheel and another in the braking and acceleration system. This was his greatest achievement to date and one that he had zealously kept secret from everyone, including Billy. It would be unveiled for all the world to see for the first time in the upcoming Fourth of July parade in Red Hook, rolling along Van Brunt Street directly behind Lulu and the Veterans Post Women's Auxiliary. And no one could steal it because he had applied for a system patent just a month before. His plan was to walk along the sidewalk with the parade as he guided the radio-controlled funeral hearse along the parade route with his radio controls instead of his original idea of lying flat in the hearse and controlling it with extended controls that he was going to have Raymundo build.

The other two projects he had been working on were both viable, but this one was his baby and the one that would carry him to the elite world of respected and wealthy inventors, the great innovators who brought the world the electric light, telephone, radio, and TV. Harold saw himself joining those ranks while the Galucci family saw themselves as riding his, and Billy the Bird's, ingenuity to the top of the world.

The phone rang and when Harold answered it, he shook his head yes, smiled, and after hanging up, headed for the door.

"Hey, what are you doing?" was what he heard as he closed the door. Sylvio had Harold's voice down cold.

"Here it is, Harold," Billy crowed as he waved the remote device in front of himself.

"It works."

"And you know that how, Billy? How do you know that without testing it with the spring?"

"I could hear the mechanism click every time I pushed the button. Now all we need is to hook up the springs and let her rip."

"Okay. It's time. Let's go do that later this evening. I'll come by and get you at the candy store." They were nearing the manifestation of what they had been working on for two years on and off, and now the end product was about to emerge. Or so they hoped. But the Galuccis had other plans.

The sun was setting, masked by the rainclouds that were emptying over Red Hook. Even though it was well into spring, that evening was damp and chilly as Pat and Junior sat surveilling the O'Reilly Funeral Home. There was some light coming from inside, which gave them the thought that someone was still there.

Inside, the phone rang. As Harold answered, he was greeted by "Mr. O'Reilly, this is Louis Bradley of Canton Convertible Couches calling."

"Well, hello, Mr. Bradley. How nice of you to call. I've been hoping you would."

"Harold. May I call you that?"

"Certainly. What can I do for you?"

"Let me cut to the chase. I am reacting to your letter of inquiry regarding your claim to have invented an automatically opening and closing device for convertible sofas and full couches, and I find this intriguing."

"I'm glad you do, Mr. Bradley. My partner and I are getting ready to roll out a test model."

"When is that?"

"Within the next two weeks or so."

"And where will this rollout take place?"

"At my place here in Brooklyn."

"I would be very interested in seeing a demonstration, Harold. Can we say that will be possible? And if it turns out to be something feasible, would you and your partner be willing to negotiate a deal with me?"

"Anything is possible, Mr. Bradley. I will inform my partner of your interest, and I am certain he will agree with accommodating you. As will I."

Bradley gave Harold his contact information and they agreed to Harold and Billy calling him the next day to make plans for the demonstration. Harold was beside himself with excitement. This was a dream coming true, and he wanted to be certain that everything was planned out perfectly. He dialed Billy's number and told him the news. He expected Billy to jump through the phone as his reaction, but that didn't happen.

"What's wrong, Billy? Why ain't you jumping up and down with this? I thought you'd be running up and down Van Brunt, shouting the news. What's wrong?"

"Harold, I gotta tell you somethin' that you ain't gonna like, and I'm sorry."

Harold was growing concerned with Billy's words.

"Today, I was told that the don wanted to see me."

"Galucci?"

"Who else? He knows about our invention and he wants in." Billy was distraught as his words gushed out. "He doesn't only want in—he's talking like he's already in."

"Piss on him, Billy. What a pair of balls. What gives him the right to say that? To think that? This is our thing and ours alone."

"I know, Harold, but I gotta take some of the blame for this. It goes back to when I screwed up his gambling operation with my homing pigeons flying to the police precinct instead of his yard. The cops shut him down, and he almost went to jail, even. I screwed up big time in his eyes, but it wasn't my fault. But that don't matter with him. I screwed up and now I owe him. He's calling in that marker."

"So now you feel that you owe him a piece of our business?"

"Yeah, I guess I do. And he ain't no one to mess around with, Harold. He can get people hurt bad."

"That pissant son of his is a winner too." Harold was furious. "Geez, Billy, why didn't you tell me about this sooner?"

"I thought I could somehow make it go away. I thought maybe

we could act like the device didn't work and then we could bullshit him to something else. Like what we talked about with the bug-killing machine."

"Hell, that's something that we are working on next. Why would we want his ass in that?"

"I don't know, Harold. I made things real complicated I guess, and I'm sorry. Real sorry."

"We have to talk this through, but we have the best opportunity of our lives now, and Galucci's not going to get in the way," Harold said defiantly.

"I hope not. I sure hope not."

"Let me sleep on this and see if I can come up with something."

Billy struggled with what he had to say next. "The don said he wants to see you and me tomorrow morning. No ifs, ands, or buts."

"What?"

"Yeah, that's what he told me."

"That's bullshit, Billy. He's trying to set up an ultimatum with this." Harold looked down, deep in thought, trying to come up with a way to prevent this meeting and buy them some time.

"What's an 'ultimatum'?" Billy asked.

"It means being painted into a corner." Harold continued thoughtfully, "Here's what you tell him: I've been brought on board by the mayor's office to assist in keeping dead bodies intact during murder investigations. You know, by keeping them iced enough so they don't disintegrate."

"Hey, congratulations, Harold. I didn't know that you knew the mayor." Billy grinned as he spoke.

"No, asshole. I don't know the mayor, and that's only a story we use to delay the meeting. It will also give us some cover because he'll think I do." Harold emphasized, "I'm counting on you convincing him, Billy. This will make him back off."

"I think I can do that, Harold. I'm real sorry I caused this to happen."

"I know that, Billy. Let's work this out, but please don't keep anything else from me. Okay?"

"Okay. I'll see you tomorrow." Billy hung up, somewhat relieved.

The head of the Galucci crime family was, of course, the don, and the capos were his enforcers. Between him and them was his son Pat, who was next in line to the mob throne. This made for an interesting dynamic, as Pat was becoming more and more active in the daily business. Under some circumstances, this could be a good thing and not so good under others. The thing Pat wanted more than anything else was his father's approval, and he was hell-bent on making that happen by taking over the task of bringing Harold in line with his father's wishes. He also had some loyalty from the capos because of the fact that someday he would be the boss.

He took one of his father's capos aside and told him of an idea he had running through his head about scaring Willie the Cabbie into "forgetting" his seeing him and Junior spying on Harold O'Reilly and his experiments. And then he'd talk with Shackles the Cop about it. This could seriously hurt the possibility of their walking away with this invention, which would make his father seriously unhappy with him.

"Ya know, Pat, your father ain't gonna be happy with me if I do somethin' without his okay." Carmine Scarpino, one of Don Galucci's most trusted members of his "family," was having some grief with Pat's request. He liked Pat and had watched him grow up from a little kid to the mound of flesh he had become. He knew what a conniver Pat could be.

And he was also hearing about Shackles trying to make detective third grade by making a case big enough to get him that promotion. The word on the street was that Shackles was looking at the Galuccis and figuring that he could get them on something that could make his case for becoming a detective. "You may be playing with fire with all this, so be careful. Real careful. That's all I'm gonna say." With that, he turned his back on his future boss and walked away.

But he hadn't gotten twenty feet when he heard Pat say, "I'll remember that, Carmine. Someday this may mean something to you, and I got a real good memory."

Carmine stopped and looked down, let go a breath of surrender, and said without turning around, "I'm listening. And what is it that you got on your mind?"

"I got something that will be a way to solve a big problem for us and then, a ways down the road, make us all rich."

"You don't say," Carmine muttered practically to himself, shaking his head. He frowned as he turned back toward the younger under-boss. "Whatta you got, Pat?"

"I got a plan that can't fail. I can take this whole family into legiti-macy. No more having to pay off the bulls. No more having to battle for our turf with the other families," he said confidently. "But to do this you may have to follow what I tell you to do. The old man might not agree with what it's gonna take, Carmine."

"Wait a minute, kid. You are telling me that I gotta go against the boss? You want me to go against your father?"

"No, I ain't saying that, exactly."

"Then what are you saying exactly?"

"It's like this: we have a chance to take possession of something that can change the world for a lot of others in this entire city, but even more so here in Brooklyn," Pat crowed. He went on to tell his story about the automatic convertible couch opener and closer and what a boon it would be for the Family, the people of the Hook, and the rest of Brooklyn and other parts of the city.

Carmine let it all sink in. "So how do you take possession of this, uh, invention?" He was becoming conflicted between loyalty to the don and seeing that this scheme could work, even though he thought that Pat was still a little wet behind the ears.

"What d' ya think, Carmine? Can we make this happen or what?" Pat smiled broadly, knowing that he might have gotten Carmine's attention after explaining the invention a bit more.

"Lemme think about it."

"Don't take too long with ya thinking there, Carmine. If you want in, you gotta let me know soon."

"What d' ya mean 'want in'? I'm already in. I'm part of the Family and have been since before you was born." Carmine moved his massive body toward Pat, sweat forming on his bald head. "I never went against your father ever before, and I ain't doing it now.

He's been more than a boss to me; he's been my good friend, and I don't like it that his kid is going behind his back."

Pat, sensing that he might have overstepped his bounds, immediately started backpedaling with "Look, Carmine, maybe we got a little misunderstanding going on here. I'm not doing anything that would hurt the old man. Yeah, maybe he'll be a little pissed off at first, but that will all change when the money comes rolling in. You'll see."

Carmine didn't respond. He just grunted, looked Pat up and down, then turned and walked away.

Pat knew he had just made a big mistake and had to make a dramatic move to neutralize his misstep. His mind raced as he probed for a quick cover story he could tell his father if Carmine decided to go to him about this. It didn't take long for him to come up with something, and that something was to create a need to do a hit on Willie the Cabbie.

"Pop, I gotta tell ya something," Pat muttered as he walked into his father's office.

"And what is that?" the don said as he lowered the newspaper he was reading. He tapped the ash off his cigar and leaned back in his chair.

"You know already that I heard Willie the Cabbie was in a huddle with Shackles the Cop. He was pointing toward Billy the Bird's apartment building, and he was in the cop's face like he was saying something about Billy and probably his invention. Then he points his finger in our direction."

The don released a breath of frustration and looked at his son with mild distain. "I get the impression that you have a suspicion about something that has to do with Billy the Bird. So you think that we should do what because of this?" He forced a knowing smile because he was becoming more and more aware of Pat's obsession with all things Billy the Bird.

"I don't know really, Pop." Pat shrugged his shoulders and then put his finger to his temple, indicating that he had an idea. "Maybe it's time we eliminate this problem and Willie along with it."

"What do you mean 'eliminate'?" The don kept his eyes focused on his son, who was beginning to squirm as he continued the conversation.

"It's this simple. If we take the steps that will get the bumps out of the road, then we don't have to deal with it later."

"What bumps?"

"Willie, for starters."

The don sat pondering what his son had just said for a moment. "So you think we should make Willie disappear?" He leaned forward in his chair, and Pat leaned backward in his. "Is that what you're saying?"

"Not disappear, just shaken up so he doesn't run his mouth and cause us problems. He's already talking about this with Shackles. Who else is he gonna be telling? The Pope?" He laughed with that, expecting his father to do so too.

But his father didn't laugh. He grunted in disapproval. "You got to be kidding me."

Pat stuttered back, "Look, I'm just trying to make this happen."

"Make what happen? Popping Willie? Or scaring the shit out of the poor bastard?"

"No, no nothing like that. Just getting the message across to him that he should keep his nose out of our business. That's all."

The don sat staring at his son while running what he had just heard through his mind. "What is it you think will come outta taking Willie for a ride?"

"Pop, all I'm saying is this: we pick him up at night and take him toward the Gowanus Canal, making him think about keeping his mouth shut. If he doesn't agree and show some respect to you, then maybe we gotta do what we gotta do."

"And this accomplishes what?" the don probed.

"It could be that it accomplishes no more conversations with Shackles. Then maybe Shackles loses his interest in a ride to a promotion on our backs." Pat stopped there, hoping he was reaching his father. "If Shackles pushes this far enough, it could make problems for us. Without Willie, he ain't got what he needs."

"You really believe that this could be a problem for us?"

"Yeah I do. I do." Pat sat back in his chair. "I know you like Willie, but this could be a problem that's not as big now as it could be down the road."

"You know what I think? I think that you're trying to cover your ass for making a stupid mistake by trying to off someone who doesn't need offing." The don was frustrated by his son's thinking and strategy. "I thought that when you grew up, you would start to get it."

"Get what, Pop?"

"Get your head out of your ass." The senior Galucci grinned sarcastically. "You know that if you capped Willie and make his body disappear, a lot of people will notice him gone. You get that, right?"

Pat shrugged his shoulders. "Maybe for a while. Yeah."

"Maybe for a while," the don repeated slowly and pointedly, as if he didn't believe what he had just heard from his son.

"Look, maybe it's a dumb idea."

"Maybe it's a dumb idea." Again the don repeated what he had just heard slowly, this time very pointedly.

Pat got up slowly from his chair. "I gotta go, Pop. See ya later."

"I gotta go, Pop," the don repeated his son's words slowly, almost to himself. He shook his head as he watched Pat amble slowly out of the room.

Pat knew that he had made a mistake by telling his father about how he felt Willie should be handled. The reaction he had gotten would have backed off a smarter man, but that wasn't the case with the underboss. Not by any means. He walked up to Junior, who was sitting at a table in the social club sipping his espresso while reading the *Daily News* sports page.

"Where's Louie and Tino?" Pat asked his underling as looked to his left and then right.

"I don't know." He shrugged.

"Find them for me."

Within minutes, Louie and Tino were huddling with Pat and Junior. Pat told them that he wanted them to find Willie the Cabbie and take Junior with them as a driver.

"As a driver?" Junior queried. "A driver for what? You gonna smoke this guy, boss?" He was not liking where this was going.

"No, we're just gonna get his attention so he understands that talking with cops ain't good for his health and my blood pressure." Pat chuckled. "But if he gets mouthy and doesn't seem to be coming around then you gotta do what you gotta do."

"Hey, wait a minute, Pat, you know that your father's not gonna be happy with this. He likes Willie a lot, and I heard him tell you that." He looked distraught and a bit conflicted because he had been given his orders by the don himself to keep an eye on Pat, and this was definitely something he should be reporting back to the big boss. But his ties to the underboss Pat were stronger, and that left him asking himself, "Now what?"

He thought he had better try to talk Pat out of this to try to keep himself out of ground zero when the bomb went off. He decided to try to control the situation when they had Willie in the car. Louie and Tino were younger and way below his rank in the Family. Besides, they were just muscle and light on the intelligence side of the street. He felt that he could manage the situation.

"You guys find a way to get him in the back of Junior's car at night. That should scare him just doing that. Then you two." He pointed at Louie and Tino, who were nodding their heads while smiling broadly because this was something big to them. They were finally doing something that meant a lot to the big boss's son.

They set out looking for Willie and didn't find him until early in the evening as he was just entering Michael's Restaurant and Soda Fountain at the corner of Wolcott and Van Brunt Street. "Yo, Willie. Listen, we gotta talk," Junior said before Willie could open the door.

"Sho, wha' den?" came Willie's usual response when greeting someone. He looked at Junior while awaiting a response.

"Come on over to the car where we can hang out for a few minutes." It was starting to rain, and that gave Junior an excuse to have them sit in the car as the rain turned heavy. "It's like this, Willie, we are here to give you a message from the don."

"Sho, wha' den?"

Willie was seated in the back seat between Louie and Tino, who had gotten in on either side and now each had a handgun pointed against his ribs. "Hey, what's going on here?" Willie said as he tried to move out of the car. Tino pulled him back into the position between the two guns as Junior started to drive toward the Gowanus Canal. Willie knew what that meant and he was getting scared. Very scared.

"Hold on, fellas. What you thinking Willie done?"

"What you done, Willie, was talk with the cops, and that ain't what you wanna do when you're supposed to be a friend of the don," Junior said stoically.

"What you think I was saying?" Willie asked.

"You talked with Shackles about the invention that the little Mick and the Bird are building and that the don wants to steal it. Not a good thing for you to be talking about."

"I only wanted to keep things from going off the rails for everyone, Junior. That's all. No mo'. No less. That's all."

Junior didn't answer as he drove through the darkened streets of Red Hook.

"Where we going, Junior?" Willie asked, showing more fear in his voice.

"That depends on you."

"What do that mean?" the frightened cab driver responded.

Junior waited a minute before answering. "It means that you ain't so good at keeping a secret. It means that when you're a friend of the don, you ain't friends with no cops."

"Okay. Willie get that, Junior, but I was only trying to keep this from becoming a problem for him because I thought that Pat was gonna cause a problem for him."

"So you thought that by causing a problem for his son you was gonna protect him?"

Willie spurted, "Yeah. That's all it be. I promise ya." He let out a sigh.

"That's all it be," Junior repeated. "Well, let me tell you, Willie, if that's all it was, it was enough to get you snuffed. You get me?"

"Sho, wha' den?"

"What then, Willie? What then? What the hell do you think what then?" Junior hit the brakes on the car as they entered the first of two empty streets before they got to the Gowanus Canal. Louie and Tino took that as signal to shoot. Willie took it the same.

As they both pulled the triggers, Willie moved forward, pushing

Junior's head into the steering wheel as Louie and Tino shot each other and screamed in pain. Willie jumped out of the car and high-tailed it for an alleyway behind two houses.

Junior recovered and turned to see his two underlings writhing in pain and the rear door flung wide open. "Shit," was all he could say as Willie disappeared into the night and from the neighborhood. He got out of the running car, hoping to see where Willie went, but he was gone. "Shit, shit, shit!" was all he was capable of saying at that moment.

He got back in the car and sped away toward Doc Regondo's place, the mob doctor who did special favors for the don, to try to fix the two in the backseat who were bleeding all over his car.

SIXTEEN

You Can't Fix Stupid. Or Can You?

"So you see, boss, it was all a kinda freaking accident. I hope this doesn't screw up your deal. I mean it, boss. Willie wasn't cooperating with us, and I figured he needed some more coaching. And that's why we headed toward the canal."

"What kinda coaching were you figuring on doing?" The don was seething with anger because he knew that this was going to be a major problem for him. "How could you be so stupid to do this without coming to me first?"

"I didn't want to bother you, boss. You got enough on your plate already."

"I got enough on my plate? I got enough on my plate? Between you and my asshole son, it's a wonder I even got a plate at all." The don's face was crimson and his eyes were filled with fury.

"I'm sorry, boss. I know this was a bonehead thing to do. It won't happen again." He hung his head as he spoke practically in a whisper.

"You can bet your sweet ass that it won't happen again. Now get outta my sight." The don turned his back on Junior and drew a deep drag on his cigar as he searched for a way to tamp down what could become a problem if the cops caught wind of Willie being taken for a ride. After a few moments, his anger subsided, and he thought about trying to find Willie and convince him that he had not put a hit out on him. He would tell him that Junior was only "playing" with him and it was all a joke. He knew that Willie was gullible, but he was no fool and shouldn't be played that way. He thought about handling this one himself because Willie and he had a friendship that went back years but had weakened when he became the don of the Galucci crime family. Due to his having to move into the realm of what is known as the "boss," he had to become almost untouchable, and that affected old friends. But Willie, being the person he always was, was forgiving and could be talked out of acting foolish.

Don Galucci picked up the phone and called Carmine Scarpino. He told the big capo that he wanted him to go find Willie the Cabbie and tell him that he was okay with the don, who only just found out about the "joke" Junior and his friends played on him. The message also included an invitation for Willie to stop by his favorite bakery on President Street and pick up whatever pastries he wanted and bill it to Don Galucci.

Carmine asked, "Boss, is there anything I need to know about this?"

"Uh, it's about getting the piss scared outta him by Junior and some of the boys. You ain't heard yet about Louie and Tino shooting each other?"

"What? They got a beef with each other?"

"No, nothin' like that." The don went on to explain that they shot one another in the hands and bled all over Junior's car. Served him right for being a *cretino*. "I don't know where they got the idea to pull this shit."

"I do," Carmine mumbled without thinking.

"What do ya mean, 'you do'?" He jumped on the capo's mumbled statement.

"Oh, nothin', boss. Just thinking out loud." He realized he shouldn't have said that.

"You wuz doin' more than thinking out loud, Carmine. Come on, don't try to bullshit me. You know better than that."

"Look, boss, there's no way I'm ever gonna be anything but upfront with you, but I'm not comfortable with causing a problem with you and the kid," Carmine said regretfully, looking down.

"What did he do now?"

"Eh, it's like this, boss. Pat mentioned somethin' to me about an invention. That if he could get his hands on it, we would be all be rich. He started to pitch it to me packaged like that."

Don Galucci bit into his cigar and said to Carmine, "This is what you do for me. You don't do anything that asshole son of mine asks you to do, and that's it! The other thing is you find Willie the Cabbie and you tell him everything is good with me and him, and I'm sorry 'bout the joke Junior played on him. It's all good."

"Where do you think he is now?" Carmine knew that he should do what he was told to do and leave the rest of it alone.

"He hangs out at the Blue Bar with his friend, a guy named Richard. Get going. I got to put out a fire."

What they didn't know was that Willie the Cabbie was on his way to his sister's house in the Bronx and had no plans to ever go back to Red Hook. And something else that they didn't know was that Harold was on a mission to teach Fat Pat a big lesson about not trying to take something he had been working on for a long time and using it to make himself rich.

SEVENTEEN

Are You Kidding Me?

_____

"So, Harol', Billy was asking me about fabricatin' some rods for your car so you can drive it laying flat down. You know I can do somethin' that could work like that, but why you want to do it?" Raymundo asked while watching Harold feed sunflower seeds to Sylvio.

"Actually, Raymundo, it's like this: what Billy was trying to get across to you was more like developing a different kind of metal alloy that could make a very powerfully expandable spring. But, my friend, I believe we might have got that done. The thing about the rods and the car came up later. But I think we have another way to get that done too."

"Then why are you an' me talking, Harol'?"

"Because I'm not sure if we got it right yet. And I want to make sure because there's a lot riding on all this." Harold took his attention from Sylvio and turned it toward Raymundo.

Raymundo took a breath. "I still don't know why we're talking, then."

Harold told Raymundo about the opening-and-closing device without getting too far into the details. "What I need here is the strongest and, at the same time, most flexible spring on earth. I know it may sound crazy to you, but you follow me?"

Raymundo tried to wrap his head around it. "How do you know you got that when you get it?"

"That's the big question, and unless we have the exact answer, the whole thing could fail." Harold was unusually pensive.

"So what do you wan' me to do, Harol'?"

"I'd like you to take a shot at making us the spring that can get this done. If you do, we'll cut you in for ten percent. Flat out."

"Ten percen' of what?"

"Of the deal, Raymundo. The whole deal."

"Wow. I don' know what to say." Raymundo smiled broadly when he fully realized what was going on.

"But that only happens if you can deliver the goods. We got an understanding here?"

"Yeah. Okay, I guess." Raymundo was going up and down emotionally.

"I hope you can do this. Here's the spring I came up with. Let's see what you can do. And oh yeah, I may be talking with you about something else I may be needing some assistance on."

"Like what, Harol'?"

"Maybe a secret installation job onto the car of a major asshole. It's a joke I want to play on someone."

Raymundo smiled and flipped the spring in his hand a couple of times, then looked it over before putting it in his pocket and heading out the door of the funeral parlor onto King Street.

Billy phoned Harold. "Hey, I think I got a way out of this mess with Don Galucci without pissing him off."

"And how would that be, Billy?"

"You and me meet with him tomorrow like he wants, and we tell him that we had already cut a deal with a company that we can't talk about with anybody—and it includes Shackles the Cop."

"And you think this will not piss him off? How?"

"For some reason he fears Shackles. I don't know. Then we hit him with this: we cut him in on the bug-killer fifty-fifty. Just him and us."

Harold paused for a minute. "Billy, do you really think he's that stupid? He would go for that fish story?"

"But it ain't no fish story, Harold. This is something that we might really be able to pull off. All we need for starters is some electric grills, a pile of dog shit, and a big fan."

Harold laughed from his feet up to his head. "I get it. Like we joked about with John that day and got Fat Pat all caught up in it, believing we were serious."

"Yeah, but it ain't no joke. This is something that we can pull off easy. We don't got to do anything but buy what we need for starters and get him involved from the start, then we build it from there. We set up a demonstration in the empty lot across the street from John and Mary's, where half the neighborhood takes their dogs to crap. By mid-summer there are more flies there than in a jungle."

"I don't see it working enough to fool him, but it may buy us some time. Yeah, it may just buy the time we need." Harold smiled.

"It will. It's a natural, and it could turn into something that can get him off our ass. Go with me on this."

"I know what you're doing here, Billy, but I don't like who you're doing it with, and if he gets the feeling that you're screwing with him, it could bad. Really bad."

"But we ain't screwing with him; we are offering him a clean deal without any involvement of other people. This could work and turn into something very big too. Think about it that way, an' I bet it can get us out of this friggin' jam I put us in."

Despite his reservations about getting too involved with the don, Harold saw it as a possible part of his plan to get even with that fat bastard son of his.

———

The next morning, Billy and Harold filed into the Galucci Family Social Club and were greeted with an offer of espresso with a lemon peel. Billy accepted the offer but Harold waved it off.

Billy talked fast and explained what was going on with the couch-opener deal. The don, at first, wouldn't even listen to the story until Shackles the Cop's name entered the conversation. Things suddenly calmed down almost as quickly as they had arisen. Then the concept of the bug-killer came up and a more serious conversation ensued, much to Harold's surprise.

They talked about the lot on Van Brunt Street for the demonstration experiment of the concept and doing it during July in the height of the fly season in Red Hook. If it worked as well as Billy thought it would, then they could begin putting the concept into motion by developing it into something packageable and saleable.

As they left the meeting, laughing and relieved, they weren't aware of the furious eyes upon them and the smoke coming out of Pat Galucci's ears as he watched them.

He thought, "This ain't over." He was going to get this all back on track, and it was going to be done his way. One way or another.

EIGHTEEN

Going Against the Family

"Junior, you an' me have got work to do, and we got to do it now."
Pat Galucci sat behind the wheel of his Caddy as he ran a plan
through his head.

"An' what is that, boss?"

"We gotta find the thing that Billy has that causes the whole thing
to work."

"What thing is that?"

"The thing. The thing. The clicker." Pat waved his hands around,
as if their motion would help him figure out where the Bird was
stashing the clicker.

"I know what you mean, but I'm not sure I know what you
mean."

"I can't believe I'm hearing what I'm hearing. You know what I
mean, but you're not sure you know what I mean?" Pat was really
upset and in no mood for Junior's, or anyone else's, what he considered dumb remarks. "You gotta think before you speak, Junior." He
tapped his forehead. "Like me. Like I do."

"Okay, boss. So what do you want me to do?" Junior was getting
unhappy with the way Pat talked down to him, which was almost all
the time lately. He was reaching the point of not giving a crap about
what Pat wanted. He was tired of being treated like a dog.

"If we can get that device in my hand, that's all it will take to make this all happen. That's all it will take." The young gangster rubbed his chin as he looked from side to side, trying to come up with a hint about the place where the device could be. He now realized that this great opportunity was slipping away, and the only chance he had of keeping his plan intact was to find the thing that made the couch open and close. What he didn't know was that there were other important factors in the mix: the motor and the receiver, which were intricate parts of the process.

"So what we are looking for is a device?" Junior spoke slowly and almost in a whisper.

"Yeah."

"And what does it look like?"

This exasperated Pat to no end. "And how am I supposed to know that? You think I'm a mind reader?"

"No, I think you're an asshole." Junior half smiled to himself as that thought passed through his mind.

"Let's go," Pat ordered.

"Where are we going, boss?"

"To find the friggin' thing. The friggin' thing, Junior."

Pat threw the car into gear and headed for Van Brunt Street, where Billy the Bird lay his head every night. "We gotta get in his apartment again, Junior. We ain't got time to lose. Ain't got no time."

Van Brunt Street was partially paved with cobblestones, which caused the car to bounce quite a bit. Pat was in a hurry and he didn't mind the bouncing. But Junior did, especially after his head hit the ceiling twice. "Boss, please slow down a little before my head goes through the roof."

"Live with it."

They pulled up in front of Billy's apartment building. Then Pat realized that he shouldn't leave his car there in case someone would put together that he was burglarizing the Guarino's apartment. He pulled his car onto Coffey Street and rolled halfway down the block, where he found a place to park.

They walked quickly back up the block to Van Brunt Street and into the lobby of the building. Pat pushed the button to Billy's apartment. No answer. He pushed it again. No answer, so they made their way up to the roof and climbed onto the fire escape, then went down to the open kitchen window of the Guarino's apartment, where the curtains were halfway outside and blowing in the breeze.

Junior was nudged by his boss to climb through the window. Pat followed him clumsily and fell as he set his foot in.

"You okay, boss?" Junior laughed as he asked.

"What d' ya mean, am I okay? Why wouldn't I be?"

"Oh, nothing. I just thought maybe you got hurt when you fell."

"What d' ya mean fell? I didn't fall. What are ya, seeing things? Let's get busy quick."

They inched their way through the apartment into the living room. Junior picked up a fancy cigarette lighter that was imbedded in a porcelain elephant. "What d' ya think about this?" He showed it to Pat.

"What do I think about what?"

"This!" Junior flicked it and a flame appeared. "I guess it ain't what we're looking for."

Pat stopped in place and leered at Junior. "How dumb can you be? I keep telling you that we ain't got no time for anything but finding the device." Pat was feeling the pressure from realizing that his dream of being rich could be coming to an abrupt end.

"I'm trying. I'm trying." Junior was losing his patience now.

"What are you trying? To look like an asshole?" Pat laughed sarcastically. He was losing it.

Junior was about to tell Pat to go screw himself when Pat pointed at coffee table and what was sitting on its lower shelf.

"There." He bent down and picked up a small black square with a gray button. "Maybe? Maybe this could be what we've been looking for. Let's get outta here. I think we found it."

"Ya think so?" Junior was surprised but also relieved to get out of that apartment before someone came home.

Pat clicked the button as he pointed it at the couch in the living room. When nothing happened, he tapped it a few times without the desired result.

"What are we gonna do with that, Pat?" Junior watched his boss, wondering if he was going to take it. He soon got an answer as Pat dropped it into his pocket. He then pointed at the kitchen window as he headed for it quickly. They made their way out the window and onto the fire escape, then up the ladder.

A moment later, Billy opened the apartment door, just missing Pat and Junior. He went to the refrigerator and took out a Pepsi, then went into the living room, where he plopped down on the couch and looked for the remote so he could turn on the TV. It wasn't where it usually was, on the lower shelf of the coffee table. He sat up straight and started looking around the room for it. When he couldn't find it, he expanded the search. "Weird," was all he said as he gave up the search.

"I got somethin' for you," Raymundo greeted Harold on the phone.

"Who's this?"

"It's me, Raymundo. I been working on the metal you wanted, an' I come up with somethin' that I didn't think was possible."

Harold couldn't contain his curiosity. "When do we get together on this?"

"When you want?"

"Now?"

"I'll be there in an hour."

After the call ended, Harold called Billy and asked him to come by his place for an important meeting. Billy arrived about ten minutes before Raymundo. Harold ushered him into his office. Sylvio watched them from his perch in the rafters without a sound, but he was ready to make his presence known in an instant.

"Billy, I made Raymundo an offer to join us with our project if he can come up with a spring that will fill the bill for us," Harold said quickly.

"Eh, what kinda offer, Harold?" Billy was surprised by Harold's announcement.

"I'm basing this on his being able to come up with what we need and also your conversation with him about helping us out. We need to get this done before 'you know who' gets antsy and makes a problem for us that we might not be able to handle."

"An' so what do we want to give Raymundo if he comes through?"

"Ten percent." Harold made a sign like an umpire calling a play safe in baseball.

Billy thought about it for a bit, and his thoughts were interrupted by the arrival of Raymundo.

"Hey, Harol' and Billy. Good to see you guys."

"It's good to be seen, Raymundo. Especially in my business. What do you think, Billy?" Harold sat down behind his desk as Raymundo grabbed a seat on the other side, next to Billy.

"So how did you make out with this, Raymundo?" Billy jumped right in.

Raymundo took what looked to be a bigger spring out of his pocket and raised it up for all to get a good look. "I thin' this can do it. An' maybe even do it better than we figured." He seemed confident.

"It's a bit bigger than we had planned for, but if it can do what we need, it won't be hard to adjust the placement in the couch." Harold's eyes were now sparkling as he realized that maybe, just maybe, they were closing in on the final product.

"I played with the torque a lot, and the one that you gave was too strong. It coulda sent someone into space if they were sitting on it when it opened." Raymundo laughed a bit with his words. "This one will be more easy to control and will keep things the way you want them to be." He handed over the spring Harold had originally given him, and Billy reached for it and put it in his lap as they continued talking.

"So what we do now is have you make another one of these for the other side of the couch, and we'll give it a go." Harold was cooking with all burners at that point. "Now I got another thing I would like you to work on fabricating."

"What's that, Harol'?" Raymundo asked.

"Yeah, what's that?" Billy was really curious at this point.

"I got something I want to play on Fat Pat. But let me ask you, Raymundo, if you think it will be possible. It will be the funniest thing to ever hit Red Hook."

"What is it?"

Harold explained that he would like to replace Pat's Cadillac's suspension system with springs that would cause the car to continue bouncing almost without stopping after hitting one bump. He asked if Raymundo could fabricate something like that. This idea fed Harold's impish sense of humor and desire to get even with Pat. "That's just part of it. The other part is to get someone who can grab the car overnight, change the springs out and then get the car back to where it was without there being any indication it was ever moved."

"I don't know, Harol'. That's a tall order. First of all, we're messing with the son of a don and then the police could get involved. But ya know what, I think that jerk needs to be brought down to size. I like it."

"So you'll help out with this?"

Raymundo stayed silent for a moment while he mulled over what he might be taking on and what could happen if he were caught doing it. "I don't know." He paused again for a moment. "Can I bring anyone else into this?"

"Into what? Our partnership deal?" Harold responded quickly.

"No. I'm talking about taking the kid's car and putting in new springs."

Harold ran it through his head. "I think that if you are talking about people who can keep their mouths shut"—he shrugged his shoulders—"why not? After all we're only playing a joke here. Not stealing the car, just making a few adjustments to it."

"Okay, Harol', we got a deal. But I'm going to have to pay these guys something for doing this."

"I'll cover it if it's not too crazy. Amount-wise."

"Lemme get started on the springs themselves first and see what we got when I'm done." Raymundo left, and Sylvio never said a word—but he listened closely.

NINETEEN

The Best of the Best and the Worst of the Worst

Pat Galucci and Junior were busy measuring the convertible couch in the living room of his parents' home. Junior opened and closed it manually while Pat, lying on the floor, watched the mechanism as it cycled through the opening and the closing. After several minutes, Pat got back up, shaking his head. "I think we need somebody who knows how to do this so we can get it right the first time."

"Got anybody in mind?"

"Yeah, there's a Puerto Rican guy who works in one of the factories in the Point who can be of use here."

"Who's that, boss?"

"Name's Raymundo." Pat thought he had solved a big problem when he was actually creating a much bigger one.

"Where's he from, this guy Raymundo?" Junior had never heard Pat mention him before.

"He's someone who works with gadgets. One of those uncertified scientists, I guess you'd call him."

"Gadgets? What kind of gadgets, boss?"

"The kind we need, Junior. The kind we need." Pat shook his head like he was on to something spectacular. "Why didn't I think of this before?"

"So you think he can put the finishing touches on this?"

"Absolutely." Pat grinned broadly. "Let's take a ride and see if we can find him at his job so we can talk about it."

They drove along Van Brunt Street past John and Mary's, turned up Beard Street, and stopped in front of Murphy's Metal Fabrication Shop. As they got out of the car, Roger Murphy was exiting the building.

"Hey, Roger, how're you doing?" Pat greeted him with a wave and then a handshake.

"I'm doing good, Pat. How's your father?"

"Yeah, he's good."

"What brings you here?" Roger asked.

"I want to talk with one of your guys, Raymundo."

"Why? You got a beef with him?" Roger expressed immediate concern.

"Oh, no. No beef, Roger. None whatsoever. I want to see if he can work with me on a thing I got going that if it turns out good, your company's gonna be rolling in dough with."

This got Roger's attention and raised his level of concern. He didn't want to insult the don's son, but he also didn't want to get involved in something illegal. "Why didn't you just come to me first, Pat? You know that Raymundo works for me. Right?"

"Yeah, I know that, Roger. I'm not trying to be disrespectful ta you. I just don't want to waste your time in case what I'm looking for isn't possible. That's all."

Roger nodded his head like he understood where Pat was coming from, but he didn't like the direction this was going. "Okay, Pat, go in and talk with Joey. He's the guy who supervises Raymundo. Tell him I said it's okay with me you talk with him." He started walking slowly toward one of the trucks parked in front of his building. "Give my best to your father."

"Sure, Roger, I'll let him know you was askin' about him."

Pat and Junior entered the building, and Roger Murphy got in his truck and headed over to John and Mary's for a cup of coffee and an onion roll. When he got there, he plopped down on the stool next to the one Billy the Bird was sitting on, drinking his coffee. "Hey, how're you doing, young man?" Roger asked.

"I'm doing good, Mister Murphy. How about you?" Billy smiled.

"What's this mister shit?" Roger chuckled.

"I always call my elders mister or ma'am."

"How about this elder giving you a kick in your ass?" He nudged Billy with his elbow.

"Join the club," Billy replied.

"Who else wants to kick your ass?"

"Uh, probably Pat Galucci. At least that I know of."

"You're kidding me. I just saw him a minute ago."

"Really? Where?" Billy was always curious and concerned about Pat Galucci's location.

"He came to talk with one of my employees, Raymundo. You know him, Billy."

John chimed in. "I know him well, Roger. He stops here every morning on his way to work." He placed a coffee in front of Roger while Mary buttered his onion roll.

Billy felt a chill go up his back. "What did he want with Raymundo?"

Roger shrugged his shoulders. "He was talking about bringing him in on some bullshit thing he claims he's got going."

"Oh shit," Billy muttered to himself.

"Why are you saying that, Billy?"

"Oh, nothin'. Just thinking out loud." Billy put a dollar on the counter, and Roger handed it back to him.

"I'm buying, kid," Roger said as he slapped Billy on the back.

"Oh, thanks. I appreciate that. Good to see ya."

Billy walked quickly over to King Street and into the funeral parlor, where he found Harold doing some paperwork.

He looked up and saw the angst on Billy's face. "What's wrong?"

"How much do you trust Raymundo, Harold?"

"Not sure. Why you asking me that?"

"Because at this very moment, Pat Galucci is huddling with him about our deal."

Harold's surprise showed in his face as he leaned forward in his chair. "And where did you get this bit of information?"

"I was talking with Raymundo's boss, Roger Murphy, an' he told me."

"He told you that Galucci was with Raymundo?"

"Yeah."

Harold slammed his fist into his hand. "Son of a bitch."

"This can't be happening. Every time I turn around, that fat bastard is breathin' down my neck," Billy complained.

"Our necks," Harold corrected him quickly.

"Whatta we do now, Harold?"

"Don't know. Have to think this through." Harold sat back in his chair.

"Don't know," Sylvio echoed from his perch on the rafter above Harold's head as he looked down at Billy with one eye open.

"Hey, Sylvio, I didn't realize that you was up there." Billy winked at the cantankerous parrot.

Just then the phone rang. Harold answered it and smiled as he mouthed to Billy the word "Raymundo." He winked. "What's up? You got the spring ready for testing?"

Raymundo answered, "I got something to tell you that's gonna make you mad, an' it should. Guess who just dropped by my job to talk with me about your spring?"

"I give up. Who?"

"Pat Galucci."

"What the hell, Raymundo?" Harold did his best to act surprised.

Raymundo went on to relate that Pat Galucci needed him to make a spring, and not only that, but he was going to cut him in on a monster-big deal that would make them all rich. "This guy knows a lot more about your deal than you think, Harol'."

"Yeah I'm beginning to get that impression."

"This guy can put us all in a bad place, you know, with the don an' all." Raymundo was displaying an unusual lack of confidence.

"We cut a deal already with the don, Raymundo, but it's on another project we got going. So I don't think we have to worry about him right now."

"Oh, okay, that's good, I guess. But what about the kid?" Raymundo seemed to be a bit more relaxed.

"That's a problem we need to work on. Where did you leave it with him?"

"I tol' him I need to think about what I could do with this an' get back with him in a day or so."

"Good. That gives us some time to set up something. Let's talk later, maybe after supper this evening."

Raymundo agreed and after hanging up, Harold told Billy what Raymundo said. Then the wheels started spinning in his head about a plan that could be put in place that would not only set Pat back but also get their project finalized and ready for prime time. He rubbed his hands together as he began spelling out where they would go from there.

TWENTY

"Speaking of Which"

Raymundo answered the phone call from Harold and Billy after two rings. He had good news for them and ultimately for himself. He related that he could fabricate the springs for the "high bouncing" on Pat Galucci's Cadillac and he had a way to get them installed without moving the car by using a heavy-duty car jack from his friend's car repair shop. He said with the right crew, they could get it all done in an hour or two at most. The only thing they would have to watch out for would be the cops, who would probably wonder why they were working on a car in the middle of the night. But if he caught the time when they were cooping (sleeping in their patrol cars in the middle of the night), they wouldn't have a problem. If they were to be questioned by the police, they could use the excuse that they were doing it as a surprise birthday gift for a friend—fixing his car without him knowing.

"How much is this going to cost me?" Harold asked.

"A couple of bottles of Canadian Club and two cases of Ballantine Beer."

"That's it?" Harold was pleasantly surprised.

"I can get the springs done in about two days, and that will cost about forty dollars each. I gotta keep Murphy happy, but that's it."

Harold's mind was on overdrive at this point. "I'm thinking of a way to shut Pat down for good on the couch thing, but we're going to have to really be smooth with it all. You are going to have to play a major role in this, Raymundo. But since we're cutting you in on the deal, it's actually protecting your ass on this too."

"I get that, Harol'. So what do you think, do we do his car first and then get to the couch? Or what?"

"We need to get the car done the night before the parade that Lulu's going to be in."

"You mean the goofy woman from the Post?"

"Yeah, she's sort of flakey, but she has a good heart," Harold said warmly.

"Okay." Raymundo made a who-gives-a-shit face. "If you say so."

"So we got some time to do the car. Then you can get working on the couch. Let's set one up in my other place up near Greenwood Cemetery. I've got a couch here at the funeral parlor that's a convertible, and Billy and I can move it tonight. Maybe you can come by, and I can lay out the whole thing so we are all on the same page."

"That's good with me, Harol'. This is gonna be fun." Raymundo was really getting into the whole thing. The more he knew, the more he liked.

"Just be careful with who you're using to do the work because the Galuccis have a lot of friends who owe them favors. You get where I'm going, Raymundo?" Harold cautioned.

Raymundo responded with "Do I look worried?" at which they both chuckled, but without dismissing what could happen if Don Galucci took offense.

Harold and Billy loaded the brown convertible couch that was in the office at the funeral parlor into one of the hearses, and they drove it the ten miles to the Greenwood space that housed some of the embalming equipment Harold used.

"This is kinda heavy, Harold," Billy whined as they extricated it from the hearse.

"Yeah, I know, and it's gonna be even heavier when we get it set up."

They walked it into the back of the open garage area, with Billy grunting every step of the way and Harold ignoring him. They set it down right under the window that Pat Galucci had used to spy on them. Twenty minutes later, Raymundo knocked on the door.

"I'm here, guys. Let's try 'n' do this fast. I gotta early rise in the mornin'."

Billy explained his part of the project and showed Raymundo, in detail, how the equipment worked and where he thought was the best place to set it up on this particular couch. Raymundo listened intently, studying each area Billy referred to. He glanced down at the flashlight he had in his tool kit, which was sitting on the floor right next to his feet. Getting down, he crawled under the opened couch and then turned on his back, using the flashlight to illuminate the whole frame.

Letting out a long breath, Raymundo pushed himself out from under the couch and stood back up. He looked Harold directly in the eye but said nothing.

Harold felt uncomfortable until he saw a slight smile on the Puerto Rican's face that grew into a big grin. "You guys really got somethin' here." Raymundo pointed with great confidence at the couch as he spoke.

"Yeah, and that's what we think too." Billy puffed up.

"How long do you feel this is going to take?" Harold asked.

"Not long, man," Raymundo replied quietly. He was confident and happy at that moment. "This thing turns out right, maybe me and Mr. Murphy will wind up being partners."

"You might not need him." Harold chuckled.

Raymundo took measurements of different areas of the couch, writing down the pertinent parts and where they would be located. He smiled broadly as he winked. "This is a really good idea, man. Really good."

"Here's a key for the door, Raymundo." Harold extended his hand, the key twirling around his fingertips.

"You don't got no ghosts here, right, Harol'?"

"Don't think so, but I can get some if you want." Harold's eyes flashed as he thought of a great way to scare off potential snoopers.

"You shittin' me?" Raymundo was thinking that he would be working in that space at night, and he wanted no surprises.

They all left at the same time, heading to their cars. Twenty minutes later, a big Cadillac passed the building and parked halfway down the block. Pat Galucci and Junior got out and moved stealthily to the area behind Harold's work building.

Pat rattled the doorknob, not expecting the door to open. It didn't, but he rattled it anyway.

"What ya thinkin', boss?" Junior stood back, watching Pat's actions.

"I'm thinking that maybe we should get Bruno 'the Key Man' over here so we can, how do you say, gain entrance?" He touched his forehead, accentuating his self-professed intelligence. "Let's go and grab a beer, and I'll call him."

One hour later, Harold returned to find Sylvio flitting around in his cage. He set a bag full of birdseed on the ground. "Who's there?" Harold repeated over and over in a gruff voice to the parrot, who stared at him without uttering a sound. He repeated the phrase until Sylvio fluttered his wings, then paced back and forth on his perch and said the phrase in a voice that completely replicated Harold's.

When the cage door was opened, Sylvio immediately came out and flew to one of the window ledges in the back of the room. Harold put some seeds and water near him and then bid him a quiet goodnight before leaving the premises. "Good night, you little pain in the ass," he found himself saying with a chuckle.

During this time, Pat and Junior were planted in a booth at a bar two blocks away from Harold's lab and Greenwood Cemetery. Pat had placed a call to Bruno the Key Man, who said he would be there within the hour. They were antsy because by now it had been two hours, but Pat knew better than to raise hell with him for being late because he was the best there was in Brooklyn at his trade.

Bruno grinned as he came through the door. He quickly found Pat and Junior in the sparsely populated bar. "What's up, guys?"

"We need you to get us into a place near the cemetery," Pat said quietly.

"What kinda place?"

"It's like a garage, but it's got a regular entrance door alongside the garage door. And there's a door in the back of it. A regular door." Pat moved his hands like he was drawing an air picture of the place.

"Where is it?"

"Follow us there. It's only a couple a' blocks." Pat grunted as he got out of the booth. He nodded his head, signaling Bruno to follow Junior and him.

They made their way back to Harold's garage lab, and Bruno went to work. Within minutes, the door was opened, and Pat and Junior prepared to enter through it. "What do I owe you, Bruno?" Pat asked.

"I'll bill ya," he said as he turned and left quickly.

Pat poked Junior and pointed at the couch sitting in the middle of the floor. "That's it, Junior. That's it. We got it. We friggin got it."

He was about to celebrate when Junior rained on his parade with "How do we know that this is the couch? We gotta find the opener."

"Look around and see what we can find."

In less than a minute, Junior found the remote control sitting on a cabinet near the couch. Pat grabbed it from Junior's hand and pressed what he thought was the control button. Nothing happened. He hit several other buttons, and still nothing happened. "This ain't makin' any sense," he carped.

"Maybe it ain't done yet, boss," Junior said cautiously because he sensed Pat's rising unhappiness. Pat just grunted in response.

"Who's there?" came a voice out of the darkness that sent them both moving rapidly toward the door, which they closed quietly as they moved back into the night.

"That son of a bitch must be sleeping there," Pat gasped as he trotted alongside Junior.

"Hope he didn't catch wind of us being there."

"Scared the shit outta me," Junior confessed, then regained his cool with "For just a second."

"I could tell."

"What do we do now, boss?"

"I don't know. Gotta figure this out now that we know that the Mick is sleeping in that place. Just knowing that gives me the creeps." Pat thought for a minute and then tapped his forehead. "I got it. I friggin' got it."

"Yeah, and what is it you got, boss?"

"Simple. We watch the Mick's movements for a couple a' days. Then we time when we can go in an' outta his place where the couch is."

"So we are gonna become spies?" Junior was loving this as he fantasized himself as some kind of an undercover government agent.

"That's what we gotta do, Junior. That's all we gotta do." Pat snapped his fingers. "And bingo, we got what we need."

"That's brilliant, boss," Junior mumbled, trying to stifle his sarcasm, which Pat did not pick up on.

TWENTY-ONE

Is This the Way It Works?

Raymundo did not waste time putting the plan of action into effect. He set up a way to change out the springs on Pat Galucci's Cadillac on the Saturday night before the parade in which Pat would be driving. In his mind, he ran through the conversation he had with Harold where he talked him out of driving his funeral hearse in the parade. "Harol', I think if you try driving your hearse in that parade the way you want, the Galuccis will put two an' two together and realize that you had somethin' to do with Pat's car. An' that would get both you an' me in a jam, man." He recalled Pat's mindset while rolling out his words.

Harold thought about it and had to agree with Raymundo, but he sure did want to try it sometime in the future. Somehow he knew that he would.

The parade was now three days away, and the changing of the car springs was two days away. Raymundo had gotten a Cadillac suspension spring and used it to create a mold in its exact shape, then began melting the metals that would bring a ton of bounce to every bump Pat drove over in the Red Hook Post parade down Van Brunt Street next Sunday morning.

Three different types of metal arrived at Murphy's shop three days before the parade, and Raymundo got busy mixing them as soon as they all arrived. He wasn't quite certain how the mixture components would work, so he began the process of combining them in equal amounts for the first batch. Then he adjusted the mixture in the next two batches. The first batch was for the couch, with him using a standard mold for convertible couch springs. It took about two hours to be cool enough to take them out of the molds. The rest of that batch he poured into the four molds of the suspension springs for the Cadillac. He labeled them according to their order of completion. Then he began the same process for the second batch, in which he changed the mixture to what he thought would bring a different, albeit only slight, result.

Harold dropped by to get a status report from Raymundo. "How's it going?" he asked, full of anticipation. "I asked the Bird to come by too."

Raymundo greeted Harold, but it was apparent that he was extremely focused on the metallic cocktail he was creating. By the time Billy the Bird arrived, Raymundo was finishing up his third mixture of the molten metallic formula and getting it ready for pouring into the waiting molds.

As Billy came through the door, he smiled. "Raymundo—and what is it?" This was a standard Red Hook greeting between the guys. No one knew why they all said, "and what is it?" and no one really cared.

"Yeah, hi, Billy." He was still focused on the springs. "I think that we got what we need here." Raymundo pointed proudly at the cooling metal in the molds.

"So where do we go from here, Raymundo?" Harold asked, his right hand holding his chin and his elbow resting on his crossed left forearm. Kind of like Ed Sullivan did on his Sunday-night TV show.

"I do some test runs on the couch. Can't do nothin' with a test on the car springs, but I think we got what we need for that."

What they weren't aware of at that moment was the car parked halfway down the block from Murphy's factory. In the car sat Pat Galucci and Junior with a pair of binoculars, watching the comings and goings.

"Son of a bitch," Junior heard Pat mutter.

"What's up, boss?"

"That no-good asshole Raymundo must be working with the Mick and Billy the Bird behind my back!"

"Why? What's going on?" Junior shifted in his seat, trying to get a better view of what Pat was seeing.

"Harold went into Murphy's a half hour ago, and now Billy the Bird just arrived."

"Oh, that ain't a good sign, boss."

"No it ain't, Einstein," Pat commented sarcastically. "No it ain't."

"Now what?"

Pat thought for a minute. "I think that we just sit and watch. If either of those bozos comes out with something in their hands, we just follow them."

"And?"

"And we watch." Pat was putting together a plan in his head that he was beginning to think might finally get him what he needed to make this all come together.

A half hour later, Harold and Billy emerged from the factory, Harold carrying a package and Billy walking alongside him. They got into Harold's car and drove off. Pat started his engine and followed them out of the Hook and to the Greenwood Cemetery space.

"I think we got 'em," Pat said with a big smile as he parked near the corner and out of sight of anyone going in or out of Harold's place. "They probably have the spring for the couch right there, an' alls we gotta do now is wait until they leave that place." He turned off the motor and took out his binoculars again.

"This is looking good, boss." Junior chuckled with the thought of what could happen for him and Pat and the entire Galucci mob if they could pull this off. He envisioned himself sitting poolside in Vegas with a bevy of good-looking women all around him. Yeah, this was what made working for Pat worth the effort. Pat was thinking about the poolside setting as well, but his vision didn't include anyone else.

Harold laid the set of couch springs he had gotten from Raymundo on a table near the couch in the center of the space.

"You think it's okay if we leave them laying out like that, Harold?" Billy pointed at the springs.

"Yeah, why not?"

"I don't know." Billy shook his head. "With Pat poking around, trying to do what he's been doing." He winced. "I don't know. I just got a bad feeling."

"We gotta leave them in a spot where Raymundo can find them when he gets here later."

"Maybe you're right." Billy was still not comfortable with this, but he felt that Harold's confidence in doing it was enough to have him go along with it.

Harold put out some more birdseed for Sylvio, who seemed to be in a quiet mood.

"I guess I should leave this here for Raymundo to use when he gets here." Billy took the remote control out of his pocket and laid it on the table.

"He already has the other one you gave him, Billy. But leave that there anyway. You never know what he would need, so let's cover all the bases."

"This is really beginning to feel like we are almost there with the couches, Harold. Now we can get rolling with the bug thing."

"Yeah, and that should be putting us back on track with the Galucci family." Harold chuckled as he spoke because in his mind that whole thing was a lark. But it could get them off his and Billy's ass, and that would be a relief. "As soon as we get this buttoned up, we can start moving on the bug project."

Pat and Junior were waiting and watching in the Caddy as Harold and Billy left the space. "Let's go to that bar we were at the other night," Pat said, starting the car. "I think we need to place another call to the Key Man."

TWENTY-TWO

This Is It!

Bruno the Key Man did his thing once again, and Pat and Junior were back inside Harold's place by the cemetery. And there sitting right in front of them was the couch and the remote control. "Ya see, Junior, what happens when you really think things through?" Pat pointed his finger at his forehead proudly.

"Ya know, boss, I gotta give it to ya. This is really something. I don't know what to say."

"Maybe you can say that I'm sort of like a genius?"

"That and then some." Junior couldn't come up with anything else, but he sure didn't think that Pat was anything but a fool.

Then Sylvio got into the act with a sudden "Who's there?" that sent both of them into a frenzy, bumping into one another.

"Harold must have come back in here when we was at the bar," Pat whispered. "Quick, let's get our asses outta here before he nails us." He grabbed the springs, the remote control, and the motor box sitting right next to it. He handed the box to Junior as they hightailed out the back door, inching it closed as they left.

They hustled down the block, jumped in the car, and flew out of there. "Now what, boss?" Junior panted as they rolled past the building without seeing Sylvio watching them from his perch on the high window.

Pat was out of breath too as he answered, "I think we can install these things on the couch in my mom and dad's living room, but we'll have to get some help with it."

"Yeah, I guess we can't use Raymundo to do it."

"I don't know about that, Junior. He may be the only game in town on it, an' I think I can convince him that it might just be a good thing for him to do it."

Junior was surprised by Pat's words. "Don't tell me that you are trusting him with something this big. Are you?"

"What d' ya think, I'm stupid or somethin'? What I'm saying here, an' pay attention, is that I get him in a position where he can't do anything but play ball with us."

"An' how do you that, boss?"

"Simple. I pay him an' his boss a visit with Deano 'the Moose' and Crazy Jerry. That should take care of any problems he has with going along with us." Deano was six foot, six inches tall and had been a professional wrestler. Jerry was nothing but crazy and everyone tried to stay out of his way. They were both members of the Galucci "family" and did whatever they were told.

"You think your father won't get wind of this, boss?"

"And how would he get wind?" Pat asked, showing some annoyance at the question.

"Well, you know your father is now in a sort of treaty with the Mick because they're working on the bug-killer thing an' all." Junior squirmed.

"And who's gonna tell him about it?" Pat looked at his underling with fire in his eyes and menace in his voice.

"Yeah, yeah, boss. I get it that there ain't no one going to bring it to his attention." Junior backed off rapidly as Pat turned his attention back to what he was going to do next. And that was a visit to Raymundo and Murphy with his two goons.

The next morning, Pat, with Junior, Deano, and Crazy Jerry in tow, parked his car in front of Murphy's place. He led the way in and was greeted by the secretary Anne Marie, who asked them if they had an appointment. "I don't need no appointment," Pat growled. "Where's Murphy?"

"Right here, Pat," Murphy said as he came through the door from the street, following them in. "What's on your mind?"

"I need ta talk with you and Raymundo. Now!" He tried to project authority in his voice.

"Sure. We can do that. Come into my office and have a seat while I go find Raymundo."

Pat directed Junior to go with him. To which Murphy responded, "I don't need any help finding him."

"Let me decide that. Go ahead, Junior. Do what I said." Pat raised his voice a bit. Deano just sat next to Pat quietly, and Jerry chuckled under his breath. Murphy shrugged his shoulders and left the room. He returned five minutes later with Raymundo and took a seat.

"Where should I sit?" Raymundo asked.

"You ain't sitting. This ain't gonna take long." Pat looked up from his chair. "You know Deano and Jerry?"

"No." Raymundo squinted when looking their way. The sun was shining through a window right behind them, making them hard to see.

"And you don't wanna know them. An' you don't gotta know them if you can keep your friggin' mouth shut an' do what I tell you to do." Pat leaned forward in his chair, and when he did, so did Jerry with a strange smile on his face.

Raymundo replied, "So tell me, Pat, just what is it you want me to do?" He didn't seem like he was anything but friendly to the young mobster, but his mind was moving quickly as he picked up on what Pat was trying to do.

"What I'm about to tell you is a big secret, and it's gonna remain that if you get my drift." Pat paused, waiting to see Raymundo's reaction. When none came, he continued. "I want you to put these springs and motor box on my father and mother's couch." He produced the springs and motor box from the bag he had sitting on the floor next to him.

Raymundo had a quizzical look on his face and shrugged his shoulders. "Yeah, I can do that."

"That's only part of it," Pat said as he rose up in his chair.

"What's the other part?"

"That you keep your mouth shut about it. You don't say shit about it to anyone."

"Who I'm gonna tell?" Raymundo acted puzzled.

"It better be no one." Pat pointed at Deano and Jerry. "Because if you do, these guys will come find you, and after that, no one's gonna be able to find you. Capeesh?"

"An' what's Mr. Murphy here got to do with this?" Raymundo was beginning to challenge Pat.

"Nothin', provided you keep your mouth shut."

"That sounds like a threat, Pat," Murphy chimed in.

"That's exactly what it is. This conversation stays in this room. You got that?"

"Wait a minute, Pat. Does your father know what you're doing here?" Murphy got up from his chair.

Pat signaled Deano, who got up and pushed Murphy back down.

"Hey, look, guys," Raymundo jumped in. "There ain't no reason for you to be pushing us around. I can do this job for you, Pat. Ain't gonna piss you off, so it gets done."

"And keep your mouth shut?"

"About what?" Raymundo responded, laughing.

"That's what I want to hear here. Then we're all on the same page. Right?"

"Sure, Pat. But I don't need you comin' in here acting like we're trying to go against you or something," Murphy explained.

Pat looked from Raymundo to Murphy and back again. "Okay. We all understand each other now."

"We always have," Raymundo said matter-of-factly. "When do you want me to put the springs on your father's couch?"

"How long do you think it will take?"

Raymundo thought for a minute. "About an hour, that's all."

"I want this to be a surprise for them, an' they'll be over at my cousin's birthday party tomorrow night, so let's say you come at aroun' eight?"

"Sure, I can be there." Raymundo smiled.

Pat grunted in response and got up and left with his goons following.

As the door closed, Murphy grabbed Raymundo by the arm. "What's going on here?"

"Nothin' for you to worry about," came the quick response.

"It don't look that way to me. I don't want you getting hurt or getting busted for doing a favor for that asshole." Murphy was upset by Pat's demeanor and threats and was thinking that he should go and talk with the don.

"Leave it alone. I got it all handled. Just relax," Raymundo reassured his boss. "We got it handled."

"Who's we, Raymundo?"

"Jus' we for now. That's all."

The parade was two days away. Well, almost, because it was already starting to be late morning. Raymundo called his crew to make sure they were ready for the next night, which was the eve of the Red Hook Post parade that would start at 9:00 a.m. sharp. Then he put the finishing touches on the car springs that had cooled in the mold that was sitting on the table in Raymundo's shop. He was smiling as he visualized Pat bouncing along Van Brunt Street as part of the parade and not being able to get out of it.

The next evening at six, Raymundo called Harold. "Hey, when do you want me to put the springs on your couch?"

"I don't know, Raymundo. I've been busy in the parlor here in the Hook and haven't been able to get over to the Greenwood space."

"I just needed ta know when so I make sure I get it done when you need it."

"Thanks, buddy. How about maybe early next week? You have the key anyway, so go ahead and do it when you have the time."

"Good. That works. I gotta go."

At eight on the nose, Raymundo rang the doorbell that was answered by Pat, who ushered him into the living room and directly to the convertible couch. "You gotta work quick. You have to get this done before my folks get home."

Raymundo laid his tools out on the floor and had the job done in less than an hour. He pushed the remote and got the couch closed as the phone rang. Pat answered it and said, "That was my father, and he called to tell me he's on his way because the party broke up early. Come on, get going." He hustled Raymundo out the door. "They're only ten minutes away."

Raymundo drove home, and the thought crossed his mind that he wasn't really sure about which set of springs he had created were the ones he had placed on the couch. Wouldn't it be funny if he had placed the weakest set instead of those that would be strong enough to open and close it.

Later that night, Raymundo's crew called him, saying that they couldn't find Pat Galucci's car. "It's not parked anywhere around his house," said Tonio, his crew leader. "What we supposed to do?"

"Stick around for a while an' see if maybe that fat asshole had a date or somethin'." Raymundo couldn't help but laugh as Tonio did the same thing.

"A date? That guy?" Tonio said through his chuckling.

"Strange thing but could happen. Just stick around for a bit longer."

"It's almost one o'clock, Raymundo. Should we stay until two or three?"

"Stay as long as you can, Tonio."

"The only place open now is this bar I'm calling you from, an' it looks like they're getting ready to close an' all."

"Do what you can. Nothin' more than that." Raymundo felt like he would be disappointing his new partners, but if it couldn't be done, then it wasn't supposed to be.

When Raymundo hung up the phone, he was doubtful that the auto-suspension springs were going to make it onto Pat Galucci's Cadillac, but his doubt was replaced the next morning by a smile in his gut and one on his face when Tonio called to tell him that Pat had gotten home an hour after his phone call. "We waited about a half hour to make sure he wasn't coming back out. It took us about an hour and a half to do the switch, but it's done."

"What did you do with the original springs?" Raymundo felt compelled to ask. He wanted to be sure that there was no evidence left lying around.

"They are in the water somewhere off the pier at the foot of Beard Street."

"Good job. I'll tighten you an' the guys up over the next few days."

"No big thing, Raymundo. They'll all be standing on Van Brunt Street when Fat Pat goes bouncing by. That will be payment enough for me, but the guys are expecting something."

"Got it covered. See you at the parade."

It was about half an hour before the parade was scheduled to start, and people were beginning to line Van Brunt Street so they could be curbside when it passed. Raymundo parked his car a block from the parade route on Richards Street and walked up to John and Mary's, where he got himself a coffee and a pack of L&Ms. "You seen Billy the Bird yet, Mary?" he asked just as Billy came through the door and sat down on the stool next to him.

"We all set?" Billy whispered.

"Yeah," Raymundo whispered back.

"Good."

"Why are we whispering?" Raymundo laughed.

"Yeah. What's the big secret?" John asked from behind the counter.

"Nothin', John. We were jus' kidding one another about somethin' stupid." Raymundo winked.

"I figured that." John smiled.

"Stand up, Raymundo," Harold said loudly as he came through the door, pulling a tape measure from his pocket. "Looks like you put on a few pounds, and I've got to keep my records up to date on all my perspective customers, ya know."

"Harol', you are one crazy son of a bitch. You know that. Right?" Raymundo almost spit his coffee out while laughing and trying to speak.

"So I've been told. But somebody has to do this job."

"Okay, everybody, please grab a folding chair from the back and get situated at the curb. We all need to be right there so we can cheer Lulu when she marches by." Mary liked to be early for everything, including the Red Hook Post parade.

One by one, each grabbed a chair and set them up outside the store. Tonio showed up, and he was given a chair too. A few minutes later, the Visitation Catholic Church marching band started playing, and although they were blocks away, the music could be heard outside as well as inside John and Mary's Brooklyn candy store. Excitement was growing, even though much of the neighborhood had seen this parade many times before.

The Women's Auxiliary, who were in formation directly behind the band and in front of the Post's honor guard, began marching in place as the drum major raised his baton and pointed it forward as he gave the command "Forward march." And the annual event of early summer in Red Hook, Brooklyn, was underway.

The Girls Scouts' float was on the first flatbed truck that started rolling, followed by the horse-drawn wagon of the old fruit peddler, followed by a truck that had a sign on both sides that read "Anthony's Bar and Grill." Then Pat Galucci fell into line behind the wheel of his prized Cadillac with his underling sitting in the passenger seat next to him. Behind his car was the neighborhood ice cream truck and behind that were about ten different floats of local significance.

Tonio stood up from his chair by the curb and motioned for Raymundo to do the same. As he did, Harold and Billy both jumped up as they all looked down Van Brunt Street at the approaching parade that had a bouncing Cadillac that was up off the ground and back down in rhythm with the drum beat. There was a kicking foot extended out the passenger-side window, and the screams of the crowd were turning into people laughing so hard many were leaning against the buildings that lined the streets of the Brooklyn neighborhood.

Meanwhile, Don Galucci, who was at home, sat on his couch with a newspaper in his lap and a cup of espresso in his hand. He didn't feel like going to the parade that day. He rather felt like just spending the day relaxing. After reading the first few pages of the *Daily News*, he decided that he would watch some television.

He fumbled around for the TV remote, but what he found first was what he thought might be a new remote that had somehow wound up on his coffee table. The morning sun was coming through the window just opposite from where he was sitting, and the glare made seeing the TV set difficult, so he got up and pulled down the shade.

The don was a happy man that day—that was until he pressed the power button on the new TV remote control.

And the following morning's headlines read "Red Hook Resident Suffers Abrasions, Glass Cuts, and a Broken Leg After Being Launched Through Living Room Window."

THE END

From the Author to You

My fondest memories of growing up in Red Hook, Brooklyn was being like part of a great, big, extended family. Everyone knew everybody, and there was a means of rapid communication that rivaled even today's social media. If I did something wrong blocks away from my house, by the time I got home there was Mom waiting for me with her wooden spoon in hand. The people in the neighborhood were working class, honest, loving, and tough. If there was trouble coming our way, it would find Red Hookers standing side by side waiting to meet it.

It was a time of magic in a place filled with people who were real characters, whose view of life was simple. I hope the characters become as alive for you as they are for me. My mind wanders back to that place and time and my mother Mary, father John, Brother Charles, and sister Linda. Morrisseys all, and every so often it brings a big smile to my face and my heart when I once again realize that there really was such a thing as the good old days.

Tom Morrissey

Made in United States
Orlando, FL
27 October 2023